DOS
FOR
DUMMIES®

Quick Reference

by Greg Harvey

IDG BOOKS

IDG Books Worldwide, Inc.

An International Data Group Company

San Mateo, California ◆ Indianapolis, Indiana ◆ Boston, Massachusetts

DOS For Dummies Quick Reference

Published by
IDG Books Worldwide, Inc.
An International Data Group Company
155 Bovet Road, Suite 310
San Mateo, CA 94402

Library of Congress Catalog Card No.: 93-78749

ISBN   1-56884-007-1

Printed in the United States of America

10 9 8 7 6 5 4 3

Distributed in the United States by IDG Books Worldwide, Inc.

Distributed in Canada by Macmillan of Canada, a Division of Canada Publishing Corporation; by Computer and Technical Books in Miami, Florida, for South America and the Caribbean; by Longman Singapore in Singapore, Malaysia, Thailand, and Korea; by Toppan Co. Ltd. in Japan; by Asia Computerworld in Hong Kong; by Woodslane Pty. Ltd. in Australia and New Zealand; and by Transword Publishers Ltd. in the U.K. and Europe.

For information on where to purchase IDG Books outside the U.S., contact Christina Turner at 415-312-0633.

For information on translations, contact Marc Jeffrey Mikulich, Foreign Rights Manager, at IDG Books Worldwide; FAX NUMBER 415-358-1260.

For sales inquiries and special prices for bulk quantities, write to the address above or call IDG Books Worldwide at 415-312-0650.

COMPUTER
BOOK SERIES
FROM IDG

is a trademark of IDG Books Worldwide, Inc.

About the author

Greg Harvey, the author of over 30 computer books, has been training business people in the use of IBM PC, DOS, and software application programs such as WordPerfect, Lotus 1-2-3, and dBASE since 1983. He has written numerous training manuals, user guides, and books for business users of software. He currently teaches Lotus 1-2-3 and dBASE courses in the Department of Information Systems at Golden Gate University in San Francisco. Harvey is the author of *Excel For Dummies, 1-2-3 For Dummies, WordPerfect For DOS For Dummies Quick Reference, Windows For Dummies Quick Reference*, and *PC World WordPerfect 6 Handbook*.

About IDG Books Worldwide

Welcome to the world of IDG Books Worldwide.

IDG Books Worldwide, Inc., is a division of International Data Group, the world's largest publisher of computer-related information and the leading global provider of information services on information technology. IDG publishes over 194 computer publications in 62 countries. Forty million people read one or more IDG publications each month.

If you use personal computers, IDG Books is committed to publishing quality books that meet your needs. We rely on our extensive network of publications, including such leading periodicals as *Macworld*, *InfoWorld*, *PC World*, *Computerworld*, *Publish*, *Network World*, and *SunWorld*, to help us make informed and timely decisions in creating useful computer books that meet your needs.

Every IDG book strives to bring extra value and skill-building instruction to the reader. Our books are written by experts, with the backing of IDG periodicals, and with careful thought devoted to issues such as audience, interior design, use of icons, and illustrations. Our editorial staff is a careful mix of high-tech journalists and experienced book people. Our close contact with the makers of computer products helps ensure accuracy and thorough coverage. Our heavy use of personal computers at every step in production means we can deliver books in the most timely manner.

We are delivering books of high quality at competitive prices on topics customers want. At IDG, we believe in quality, and we have been delivering quality for over 25 years. You'll find no better book on a subject than an IDG book.

John Kilcullen
President and C.E.O.
IDG Books Worldwide, Inc.

IDG Books Worldwide, Inc. is a division of International Data Group. The officers are Patrick J. McGovern, Founder and Board Chairman; Walter Boyd, President. International Data Group's publications include: **ARGENTINA's** Computerworld Argentina, InfoWorld Argentina; **ASIA's** Computerworld Hong Kong, PC World Hong Kong, Computerworld Southeast Asia, PC World Singapore, Computerworld Malaysia, PC World Malaysia; **AUSTRALIA's** Computerworld Australia, Australian PC World, Australian Macworld, Network World, Reseller, IDG Sources; **AUSTRIA's** Computerwelt Oesterreich, PC Test; **BRAZIL's** Computerworld, Mundo IBM, Mundo Unix, PC World, Publish; **BULGARIA's** Computerworld Bulgaria, Ediworld, PC & Mac World Bulgaria; **CANADA's** Direct Access, Graduate Computerworld, InfoCanada, Network World Canada; **CHILE's** Computerworld, Informatica; **COLOMBIA's** Computerworld Colombia; **CZECH REPUBLIC's** Computerworld, Elektronika, PC World; **DENMARK's** CAD/CAM WORLD, Communications World, Computerworld Danmark, LOTUS World, Macintosh Produktkatalog, Macworld Danmark, PC World Danmark, PC World Produktguide, Windows World; **ECUADOR's** PC World; **EGYPT's** Computerworld (CW) Middle East, PC World Middle East; **FINLAND's** MikroPC, Tietoviikko, Tietoverkko; **FRANCE's** Distributique, GOLDEN MAC, InfoPC, Languages & Systems, Le Guide du Monde Informatique, Le Monde Informatique, Telecoms & Reseaux; **GERMANY's** Computerwoche, Computerwoche Focus, Computerwoche Extra, Computerwoche Karriere, Information Management, Macwelt, Netzwelt, PC Welt, PC Woche, Publish, Unit; **HUNGARY's** Alaplap, Computerworld SZT, PC World, ; **INDIA's** Computers & Communications; **ISRAEL's** Computerworld Israel, PC World Israel; **ITALY's** Computerworld Italia, Lotus Magazine, Macworld Italia, Networking Italia, PC World Italia; **JAPAN's** Computerworld Japan, Macworld Japan, SunWorld Japan, Windows World; **KENYA's** East African Computer News; **KOREA's** Computerworld Korea, Macworld Korea, PC World Korea; **MEXICO's** Compu Edicion, Compu Manufactura, Computacion/Punto de Venta, Computerworld Mexico, MacWorld, Mundo Unix, PC World, Windows; **THE NETHERLAND'S** Computer! Totaal, LAN Magazine, MacWorld; **NEW ZEALAND's** Computer Listings, Computerworld New Zealand, New Zealand PC World; **NIGERIA's** PC World Africa; **NORWAY's** Computerworld Norge, C/World, Lotusworld Norge, Macworld Norge, Networld, PC World Ekspress, PC World Norge, PC World's Product Guide, Publish World, Student Data, Unix World, Windowsworld, IDG Direct Response; **PANAMA's** PC World; **PERU's** Computerworld Peru, PC World; **PEOPLES REPUBLIC OF CHINA's** China Computerworld, PC World China, Electronics International, China Network World; **IDG HIGH TECH BEIJING's** New Product World; **IDG SHENZHEN's** Computer News Digest; **PHILLIPPINES'** Computerworld, PC World; **POLAND's** Computerworld Poland, PC World/Komputer; **PORTUGAL's** Cerebro/PC World, Correio Informatico/Computerworld, MacIn; **ROMANIA's** PC World; **RUSSIA's** Computerworld-Moscow, Mir-PC, Sety; **SLOVENIA's** Monitor Magazine; **SOUTH AFRICA's** Computing S.A.; **SPAIN's** Amiga World, Computerworld Espana, Communicaciones World, Macworld Espana, NeXTWORLD, PC World Espana, Publish, Sunworld; **SWEDEN's** Attack, ComputerSweden, Corporate Computing, Lokala Natverk/ LAN, Lotus World, MAC&PC, Macworld, Mikrodatorn, PC World, Publishing & Design (CAP), Datalngenjoren, Maxi Data, Windows World; **SWITZERLAND's** Computerworld Schweiz, Macworld Schweiz, PC & Workstation; **TAIWAN's** Computerworld Taiwan, Global Computer Express, PC World Taiwan; **THAILAND's** Thai Computerworld; **TURKEY's** Computerworld Monitor, Macworld Turkiye, PC World Turkiye; **UNITED KINGDOM's** Lotus Magazine, Macworld, Sunworld; **UNITED STATES'** AmigaWorld, Cable in the Classroom, CD Review, CIO, Computerworld, Desktop Video World, DOS Resource Guide, Electronic News, Federal Computer Week, Federal Integrator, GamePro, IDG Books, InfoWorld, InfoWorld Direct, Laser Event, Macworld, Multimedia World, Network World, NeXTWORLD, PC Games, PC Letter, PC World Publish, Sumeria, SunWorld, SWATPro, Video Event; **VENEZUELA's** Computerworld Venezuela, MicroComputerworld Venezuela; **VIETNAM's** PC World Vietnam

Acknowledgments

I am indebted to a number of people on this project — how was I supposed to know that the Bills would fold up on their third Super Bowl try? Seriously, I want to thank all of the following people who worked so hard in various and sundry (and sometimes, even mysterious) ways to make this book a reality:

David Solomon and John Kilcullen for their support for this "baby" Dummies book.

Brandon Nordin and Milissa Koloski for coming up with the original concept of a DOS command reference for the rest of us.

Janna Custer and Megg Bonar for straightening out all the contract details.

Diane Steele for editing the hell out of this manuscript (some parts required a little more Exorcism than others) and supporting me through yet another project. (Diane, you're so good you make writing about DOS fun! Well, almost.)

Bill Hatfield for the tech review, Tricia Reynolds for editorial support, Beth Jenkins and Cindy Phipps for layout and proofreading, Jeremy Judson for *DOS For Dummies* resources, and Peppy White for the design.

Last, but never least, I want to acknowledge my indebtedness to Dan Gookin whose vision, sardonic wit, and (sometimes) good humor produced *DOS For Dummies*, the "Mother" of all Dummies books. Thanks for the inspiration and the book that made it all possible, Dan.

Greg Harvey
February, 1993
Inverness, California

(The publisher would like to give special thanks to Patrick J. McGovern, without whom this book would not have been possible.)

Credits

Publisher
David Solomon

Acquisitions Editor
Janna Custer

Managing Editor
Mary Bednarek

Project Editor
Diane Graves Steele

Editor
Patricia R. Reynolds

Technical Reviewers
Bill Hatfield
Keith Hatfield

Production Manager
Beth J. Baker

Production Coordinator
Cindy L. Phipps

Production Staff
Joseph A. Augsburger
Mary Breidenbach
Drew R. Moore

Proofreader
Charles A. Hutchinson

Indexer
Anne Leach

Book Design
Peppy White
(University Graphics, Palo Alto, California)

Table of Contents

Introduction

DOS, an operating system only someone else's mother could love

Welcome to the *DOS For Dummies Quick Reference,* a quick reference that looks at the lighter side of DOS commands (such as it is). I mean, who could take seriously a command like

```
DEFRAG [drive:] [/f] [/s[:]order] [/b]
[/skiphigh] [lcd | /bw | /go] [/h]
```

a new DOS 6 command for optimizing disk performance? *Defrag* and *skiphigh* sound like words right out of a Pentagon code book. And look at all those /f and /s doodads. About the only thing that seems halfway intelligible here is the /go business as in "let's get outta here." To paraphrase the great comic, "Take my DOS, *please!*"

Ah, if only DOS were really just a laughing matter! Much as we may poke fun at the DOS vocabulary, grammar, and syntax (DOS is such an easy target, kinda' like a politician), we've all heard tell of the disastrous results of misusing common commands like FORMAT or ERASE. And these major and minor catastrophes with DOS often come about as the result of little errors, perhaps as small as a misplaced star (*) or space in the command, a typo in the filename, or a semicolon where a colon ought to be.

As a means of staving off such disasters at the DOS prompt, I offer you the *DOS For Dummies Quick Reference.* This book not only gives you the lowdown on each and every DOS command — excepting DELOLDOS, FDISK, and SELECT, a trio of commands I guarantee you'll never miss — but also rates each command with icons indicating its suitability as well as its general safety (see the "The cast of icons" later in this introduction for a sneak preview).

For convenience, this book is divided into three sections. The first section contains all the DOS commands listed in alphabetical order from APPEND to XCOPY. The second section contains all the batch commands listed in alphabetical order from @ to SHIFT. The third section contains a list of the configuration commands in alphabetical order from BREAK to SWITCHES.

Regardless of what section you find it in, each command is handled in a similar way. Below the command name, replete with its suitability and safety icons, you'll find a brief description of its function. If this description reads like stereo instructions, recheck the suitability icon: this command is probably not in your league.

Below the description, you find the "DOSspeak" section (which the other quick references insist on calling the syntax). Here, you are exposed to all the gobbledygook that it takes to make this command go (please see "Parlez-vous DOSspeak" later in this introduction for decoding instructions). First, you encounter the command line and then — after you recover from that shock — you see a table explaining exactly what all that junk in the command line means.

Following the "DOSspeak" section, in most cases, you'll find a "Sample" section that gives you some examples of how you might use this command in real life. A cast of characters, which includes folks like Cousin Olaf and The Boss, pop in and out of the command examples found in the "Sample" section.

Bringing up the rear, the "More stuff" section is where I stick in any warnings, reminders, or other trivia that just might come in handy when you use the command.

How do I use this book?

You've all heard of on-line help. Well, just think of this book as on-side help. Keep it by your side when you're at the computer, and, *before* you try to use a DOS command that you're the least bit unsure of (like all 88 or however many there are now), look up the command in the appropriate section. Scan the entry, looking for any warnings (those bomb icons). Follow the "DOSspeak" section to compose the command at the DOS prompt, then check it over carefully, knock on wood or cross yourself (whatever's right), and press the Enter key.

Parlez-vous DOSspeak?

Remember those Little Orphan Annie decoding rings? As I understand it, those rings had little devices on the top that you could use to decode Annie's "secret" message for the week. The announcer read the secret messages at the end of the radio programs — real bogus things like "Consume vast quantities of Ovaltine" that the enemy was supposedly keen to intercept. To decode one of these gems, you wrote down the coded letters; then, at your leisure, you used the ring to turn each coded letter into English!

Don't you wish they made a Little Orphan Annie DOSspeak Decoding ring so that when you came upon a line of DOSspeak like

```
FORMAT drive: [/v[:label] [/q] [/u] [/f:size]
[/b] [/s]
```

all you had to do was dial up each of the coded parts on your ring to find out what they mean in English. (Wouldn't you be surprised to find out the secret message here is "Consume vast quantities of Microsoft products?")

Short of this mythical DOSspeak decoding ring, I have endeavored to give you all the keys you need to decode typical DOSspeak lines like the FORMAT example above. Just match the word or funny looking / thing, called a *switch*, in the DOSspeak line with the word or / thing in the table that describes each option. Doing that kind of "word-for-word" translation will give you a basic idea of what it is you're telling DOS to do when you use these things.

Along with this word-for-word translation, you need to have a rudimentary understanding of DOSspeak grammar. That's where the different typographic conventions used in the DOSspeak line come into play.

- The things you *must* include in the DOS command to get it to do anything are printed in **bold** type. If you look back at the earlier FORMAT example, you'll see that of all the many things that appear in this line, only **FORMAT** and *drive:* are required.

- Optional things in the command line are enclosed in brackets, which, by the way, you don't actually include when typing the stuff inside them at the DOS prompt.

In addition to the distinction between required (bold) and optional (nonbold enclosed in brackets) stuff, you will also find a distinction between stuff you type verbatim and stuff that you substitute with your own information.

- Stuff you type verbatim is shown in regular type.

- Stuff you replace with some other information — otherwise known as *variables* — is shown in *italics*.

Harkening back to the FORMAT example, of the two pieces of information that you have to give, **FORMAT** and *drive:*, you enter **FORMAT** verbatim (although, you don't have to capitalize the letters — this is just a typographic convention). In place of the word *drive:*, you enter the letter of the drive with the disk you want to format, such as **a:** or **b:**.

Some DOS commands make you choose between one or more alternate values. Choices between one thing or another in DOSspeak are shown by placing a | (vertical bar known as a pipe character, although it looks a lot more like a pipe cleaner) between the alternatives. For example, if you look up the VERIFY command in this book, you'll see the DOSspeak line

```
VERIFY [on | off]
```

Now, keeping in mind our DOSspeak grammar rules, only the command name **VERIFY** is absolutely essential 'cause it's in bold, while the [on | off] part is enclosed in brackets.

If you enter VERIFY all by itself, DOS tells you the current status of disk verification, that is, whether it's on or off. If, however, you want to change the status of disk verification, you must then add the on or off optional parameter to the command. You know that you must choose between one or the other and not try to enter both because there's a pipe | thingy between them. You also know that once you choose one, you must enter it verbatim because neither one is in italics. Therefore, to turn on disk verification, you enter

```
verify on
```

at the DOS prompt. To turn it off, you enter

```
verify off
```

That's about all there is to decoding either the Dead Sea Scrolls or DOSspeak command lines. With just a little bit of practice, you can be decoding your secret DOSspeak messages faster than Annie could say, "Drink your Ovaltine."

The cast of icons

In your travels with the DOS commands in this book, you'll come across the following icons:

 Recommended for your average DOS user.

 Not recommended for your average DOS user.

 Not suitable for your average DOS user, but you may get stuck having to use this command anyway.

 Safe for your data. The worst you'll end up with is another crummy error message.

 Generally safe in most circumstances unless you really don't follow instructions; then look out!

 Potentially dangerous to data but necessary in the scheme of things. Be very careful with this command. Better yet, get somebody else to do it for you.

Safe only in the hands of a programmer or some other totally DOSsed person. Stay clear unless they let you sign a release form and give you hazard pay.

Pay attention! This tip could save you some time.

Look out! There's some little something in this command that can get you into trouble (even when it's rated safe or generally safe).

Just a little note to remind you of some trivia or other that may someday save your bacon.

A handy-dandy guide to point you straight to the sections in *DOS For Dummies* where you can find more examples of how to use this command.

This command bit the dust in DOS 6 — Rest In Peace.

New in Version 6.2.

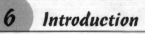

Section 1:
DOS Commands

If it just weren't for those darn DOS commands....

If you haven't already discovered it, DOS acts as though it were some kind of cantankerous Genie who only obeys your command when you phrase it *exactly* the way he expects to hear it!

This "arrogance" means that to get anything useful done with DOS commands at the system prompt (that A> or C> thing), you have to watch your Ps and Qs and mind your spaces like a hawk. In this section, you'll find an alphabetical list of all the DOS commands, indicating what the command does along with what parameters it expects (what's commonly called *syntax* in other DOS books but you and I know better as *DOSspeak*).

In addition to this kind of "essential" information, you'll find each DOS command marked with helpful icons indicating whether it's one *you* might actually use or one better left to the more "serious" (okay, nerdy) DOS user.

You'll also see icons indicating the relative safety of the command. This safety information can be *really* important because, as you learned in *DOS For Dummies,* when used improperly, some of the commands can really mess with your computer.

APPEND

Searches for data files in specified directories just as if they were in the current directory.

DOSspeak

```
APPEND [/e][/x]
```

or

```
APPEND [[drive:][path[;...]] [/x [:on | :off]
[/path:on | :off]
```

or

```
APPEND [;]
```

Variable or Option	Function
/e	(Versions 3.3+) Stores a copy of the appended search path in a DOS environment variable named APPEND. You must use this parameter the first time you give the APPEND command. Then give the APPEND command again, this time with the parameters specifying the appended search path.
/x	(Versions 3.3+) Extends the search path to include file searches and application execution. Enter this parameter only the first time you use APPEND and before you enter the parameters of the search path.
/x:on	(Versions 4+) Same as /x except that you can use it any time you give the APPEND command.
/x:off	(Versions 4+) Turns off the extended search path initiated with the /x:on parameter so that DOS applies appended directories only to requests to open files (the default setting).
/path:on	(Versions 4+) Applies the appended directories to file requests that already include a path (the default setting).
/path:off	(Versions 4+) Turns off the /path:on (default) setting.

; Separates search paths. When used alone, it cancels the search path previously set with APPEND.

If you enter APPEND without any other parameters, DOS just lists the current search path.

Sample

Let's say that you need to set the search path for data files to include the \STUFF and \NONSENSE directories on drive A as well as the \BALONEY directory on drive B. You enter

```
append a:\stuff;a:\nonsense;b:baloney
```

More stuff

APPEND pretty much does the job of the PATH command. You'll probably find PATH a lot easier to deal with.

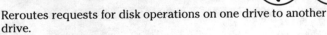

ASSIGN

Reroutes requests for disk operations on one drive to another drive.

DOSspeak

```
ASSIGN [x [:]=y[:][...]]
```

or

```
ASSIGN [/status]
```

Variable or Option	Function
x	Indicates the letter of the drive to be rerouted.
y	Indicates the letter of the drive where disk operations are rerouted to.
/status	(Versions 5+) Displays a report on the current drive assignments (can be abbreviated to /sta).

If you enter ASSIGN without any other parameters, DOS cancels any assignments currently in effect.

Sample

Let's say that you have a program which will only look for data files on drive B, but you happen to have only a floppy drive A and hard drive C. To instruct DOS to reroute all requests by the program for your nonexistent drive B to your hard drive C, you enter

```
assign b=c
```

If you have Version 4 or later, you can include the customary colons after the drive letters as follows:

```
assign b:=c:
```

More stuff

Note that the FORMAT, DISKCOPY, DISKCOMP, and SYSTEM commands ignore any disk reassignments made with ASSIGN. Only use the ASSIGN command when you are running an older application that insists on using a particular floppy drive (especially if you don't have that drive).

ATTRIB

Displays or modifies the attributes of a file. These attributes include

- whether the file is read-only (so that it can't be tampered with)

- whether the file is marked with an archive flag (used by the BACKUP and XCOPY commands)

- whether the file is a system file

- whether the file is a hidden file

DOSspeak

ATTRIB [+r | -r] [+a | -a] [+s | -s] [+h | -h]
[*drive:*][*path*]***filename*** [/s]

Variable or Option	Function
+r	Makes the file read-only so that you can't fool with it.
-r	Removes read-only status from the file so that you can fool with it.

+a	Sets the file's archive flag.
-a	Removes the file's archive flag.
+s	(Versions 5+) Sets the file's system flag.
-s	(Versions 5+) Removes the file's system flag.
+h	(Versions 5+) Hides the file so that it doesn't show up in a directory listing.
-h	(Versions 5+) Unhides the file so that it shows up in a directory listing again.
[*drive:*][*path*] *filename*	Specifies the drive, directory, and name of the file whose attributes you want to change. If the drive: and/or path parameters are omitted, DOS assumes that you mean the current drive and directory.
/s	Can be used when [*filename*] contains wildcard characters so that DOS processes matching files in all directories specified by the [*path*] parameter.

If you type *filename* after ATTRIB without using any other parameters, DOS displays the current attributes of that file.

Sample

Let's say that you're trying to delete an old version of a program from your hard disk to free up some much needed space. However, you find that you just can't get rid of one file named RESISTS.DEL that's in the current directory. To get its attribute status so that you can find out what the problem is, you enter

```
attrib resists.del
```

When you press Enter, DOS displays

```
R   C:\RESISTS.DEL
```

telling you that this baby is read-only. To change the file's attribute to "you're dog meat if I say you are," you enter

```
attrib -r resists.del
```

 See the example in *DOS For Dummies,* Chapter 3, section "The File! I Cannot Kill It!"

More stuff

Be very stingy in your use of this command. There are usually good reasons why a file comes to you read-only, carries the archive flag, is a system file, or is currently hidden from directory listings.

BACKUP

Backs up files from one disk to another.

DOSspeak

> **BACKUP** *source destination-drive:* [/s] [/m]
> [/a] [/f:[*size*]] [/d:*date*] [/t:*time*]
> [/l[:[*drive:*][*path*]*logfile*]]

Variable or Option	Function
source	Specifies the file(s), drive, or directory that you want to back up.
destination-drive:	Specifies the drive with the destination disk where the backup files are saved.
/s	Backs up the contents of all subdirectories of the *source* path.
/m	Backs up only files on the destination disk that have been modified since the last backup.
/a	Adds backup files to the destination disk (rather than replacing existing files, as is usually the case).
/f:[*size*]	Formats the destination disk if it isn't already formatted. In Version 3.3, the /f switch has no size parameter. In Versions 4+, you must specify one of the following [*size*] parameters: 160K, 180K, 320K, 360K, 720K, 1.2M, or 1.44M.
/d:*date*	Backs up only files changed on or after the specified date (*mm-dd-yy* is the default).
/t:*time*	Backs up only files changed on or after the specified time (*hh:mm:ss* is the default).

/l[:[*drive:*][*path*]*logfile*]   Creates a log file with a list of all the
                                         files that were backed up. In Versions
                                         3.2 and earlier, only the *logfile* param-
                                         eter can be used (DOS automatically
                                         saves this file in the root directory of
                                         the destination disk). In Versions 4+,
                                         you can specify the pathname with the
                                         [*drive:*][*path*] parameters. If you don't
                                         specify a pathname, DOS uses the
                                         current directory. If you don't specify a
                                         filename, DOS names the file
                                         BACKUP.LOG.

Sample

Suppose that you need to back up all the files in your \MYTURF
directory on drive C onto floppy disks in drive A (floppies that
may or may not all be formatted). In that case, you enter

```
backup c:\myturf\*.* a:/f
```

See the example in *DOS For Dummies,* Chapter 16, section
"Backing Up."

More stuff

You must use the RESTORE command (rather than the regular
COPY command) to put the files you backed up with the BACKUP
command back onto their disks and directories.

Don't use the BACKUP command to back up files under the
influence of the APPEND, ASSIGN, JOIN, or SUBST commands.

CD (or CHDIR)

Displays or changes the current directory.

DOSspeak

CD [*drive:*] [*path*]

Variable or Option	Function
drive:	Indicates the drive letter of the directory you want to make current. Note that you can't use this parameter in the CD command to log on to a new drive — to do that you simply enter the *drive:* parameter alone.

path   Indicates the name of the directory you want to make current. When the *path* parameter includes one or more subdirectories, use the \ (backslash) to separate the directory names.

If you enter CD without any parameters, DOS displays the pathname of the current directory.

Sample

Let's suppose that you're in the root directory of drive C, and you want to work with some files in the \NONJUNK directory, which is a subdirectory of your C:\MYTURF directory. To do so, you enter

```
cd \myturf\nonjunk
```

After you're done fooling with the files in \NONJUNK, you can make \MYTURF the current directory by simply entering

```
cd..
```

(the two periods take you up to the next directory level). Finally, you're ready to leave \MYTURF and want to make the root directory of the hard disk current. To do so, you either enter cd.. again to move up one level, or you can specify the root directory by entering

```
cd\
```

See the examples in *DOS For Dummies,* Chapter 16, sections "Finding the Current Directory" and "Changing Directories."

More stuff

CD is an abbreviated form of CHDIR. CHDIR does the same thing as CD and works the same way — its command name just requires more typing.

CHCP

Displays or changes the code page number, which determines the character set DOS uses to display and print characters.

DOSspeak

```
CHCP [nnn]
```

where *nnn* is a code page number as follows:

Code Page Number	Code Page Used
437	American (English)
850	Multilingual
860	Portuguese
863	French-Canadian
865	Nordic

If you omit the code page number parameter, DOS displays the current code page.

Sample

Let's say that Cousin Olaf comes to visit from Norway, and he wants to use your computer to write a letter back home. You can change the code page to Nordic by entering

```
chcp 865
```

Then, to make sure that both Olaf and your computer are now on the same code page, you can enter

```
chcp
```

and DOS displays

```
Active code page: 865
```

CHKDSK

Analyzes the allotment of storage on a disk and reports back on all kinds of interesting and not-so-interesting information, such as

- the disk's volume name and creation date
- the space occupied by different types of files and directories
- the number of bytes free and in bad sectors
- the total system memory
- a bunch of drivel about allocation units

Also reports on bits of fragmented files (known as *lost clusters in chains*) that are taking up space on the disk — which you can subsequently remove or have put into files.

DOSspeak

CHKDSK [*drive:*][*path*]*filename*] [/v] [/f]

Variable or Option	Function
[*drive:*][*path*]	Specifies the drive and directory to check.
filename	Specifies the file(s) to check for fragmentation.
/v	Displays the pathname of each file as it checks it. Be aware that on a hard disk with hundreds of files, this is one *long* report!
/f	Converts "lost clusters in chains" to files with the extension CHK if you answer Y to the prompt. Removes the lost clusters if you answer N to the prompt.

If you enter CHKDSK without any parameters, DOS analyzes and reports on the entire drive to which you're logged.

Sample

Suppose that Al in Finance gives you a floppy disk, and you want to know whether it's a high-density disk and how much free space it has. With the disk in drive A, you enter

```
chkdsk a:
```

See the examples in *DOS For Dummies,* Chapter 16, sections "Checking the Disk (the CHKDSK Command)" and "CHKDSK says I have lost files in clusters or something."

More stuff

You can't use CHKDSK on a drive under the influence of the ASSIGN, JOIN, or SUBST commands, nor can you use it to check a drive on a network.

DOS 6.2 users should use SCANDISK instead of CHKDSK.

CLS

Clears your screen of everything but the ugly DOS prompt.

DOSspeak

CLS

Sample

To get rid of all those nasty DOS error messages that have filled up the screen, you enter

```
cls
```

More stuff

You can use the CLS command both at the DOS prompt and in batch files.

COMMAND

Starts a secondary instance of the command interpreter (the part of DOS that displays prompts, interprets commands and batch files, and loads and executes application programs) by loading another copy of the COMMAND.COM file.

DOSspeak

COMMAND [[*drive:*]*path*] [*device*] [/c *string*]
[/e:*nnnnn*] [/k *filename*] [/p] [/msg] [y]

Variable or Option	Function
[*drive:*]*path*	Specifies the pathname of the directory that contains the COMMAND.COM file.
device	Specifies a character device other than the standard keyboard and monitor used for input and output.
/c *string*	Instructs the secondary command interpreter to carry out the command specified by the *string* parameter and then automatically returns control to the parent command interpreter. When you are using this switch with other parameters, the /c switch must be the last one you enter.
/e:*nnnnn*	(Versions 3.2+) Specifies the size, in *nnnnn* bytes, of the environment block for the copy of the command interpreter.
/k *filename*	Specifies the program or batch file to run and then displays the DOS prompt.
/p	Disables the EXIT command, thereby making the secondary command interpreter permanent (that is, there's no

escape back to the parent command
interpreter until you restart the machine).

/msg   Specifies that all error messages be stored
in memory (you need to use the /p switch
in order to use this one).

/y   Instructs the secondary command interpreter to step line by line through the
batch file specified by the /c or /k switch.

If you enter COMMAND without any parameters, DOS loads the
secondary command interpreter and displays the version of DOS
you're using. To remove the secondary copy of the interpreter
and return to the parent DOS interpreter, enter the EXIT command.

Sample

Just suppose that you have a batch file called BUGHUNT.BAT,
which you need to run with a secondary command interpreter (I
know it's a stretch). To do something weird like this, you enter

```
command /c bughunt
```

More stuff

See also EXIT.

If you ever do go so far as to actually use COMMAND to load a
secondary DOS command interpreter (though why you would is
unclear!), just be sure that you don't load any terminate-and-stay
resident (TSR) programs with the secondary interpreter; this
miscalculation can lead to a crash that might result in data loss!

COMP   

Compares the contents of two files to determine whether they are
identical. If they are identical, DOS indicates Files compare
OK. If they aren't, DOS indicates the location of the differences by
indicating their locations (as an offset from the beginning of the
file) along with their mismatched bytes in (of all things)
hexidecimal numbers.

DOSspeak

```
COMP [data1] [data2] [/d] [/a] [/l] [/n=number] [/c]
```

Variable or Option	Function
data1	(Versions 5+) Specifies the path and filename(s) of the first file(s) to be compared.
data2	(Versions 5+) Specifies the path and filename(s) of the file(s) to be compared with the first file(s).
/d	(Versions 5+) Displays differences as decimal numbers.
/a	(Versions 5+) Displays differences as ASCII characters.
/l	(Versions 5+) Displays the locations of differences by line number instead of offset.
/n=*number*	(Versions 5+) Specifies that only the *number* of lines in each file should be compared.
/c	(Versions 5+) Disregards differences in upper- and lowercase of ASCII characters when comparing files.

If you enter the COMP command without any parameters, DOS prompts you to enter the names of the files to be compared.

Sample

To determine whether the copy of the VITALDOC.TXT file on your floppy disk in drive A is identical to the original file in your \MYTURF directory, you enter

```
comp \myturf\vitaldoc.txt a:\vitaldoc.txt
```

More stuff

To compare specific sets of files to one another, use wildcard characters in the filenames that you enter for [*data1*] and [*data2*] parameters. If you enter only pathnames for [*data1*] and [*data2*] parameters, DOS compares all the files in directories.

COPY (Combine Files)

Combines two or more files into either the first file or a new file.

DOSspeak

```
COPY [source+source[+source]...] [destination] [/a]
[/b] [/v] [/y | /-y]
```

Variable or Option	Function
source	Specifies the drives, directories, and names of the files to be combined. Instead of individually listing the filenames separated with + signs, you can use wildcard characters in the filenames.
destination	Specifies the directory and/or name for the new file containing the combined data of the *source* files. If you omit the *destination* parameter, DOS combines all the *source* files in the series into the first *source* file listed in the command.
/a	Indicates that the *source* and/or *destination* files are ASCII (text) files.
/b	Indicates that the *source* and/or *destination* files are binary files.
/v	Verifies that the contents of the new *destination* file match the combined contents of the *source* files from which the *destination* file is created.

The /a and /b switches affect the filename that immediately precedes them in the command line as well as any filenames that follow them — until DOS encounters another /a or /b switch.

Sample

Suppose that you want to join a file called BUNK.DOC with another called HOOEY.DOC in a new third document, which is to be called TWADDLE.DOC. To do so, you enter

```
copy bunk.doc+hooey.doc twaddle.doc
```

COPY (Device to Device or File)

Copies the output of a device to a file or another device.

DOSspeak

```
COPY source destination
```

Variable or Option	Function
source	Specifies the name of the device whose output you want to copy.
destination	Specifies the file or device to which the output of the *source* device is to be copied. If *destination* is a file, you can include the path but no wildcard characters.

Sample

To copy what you type at the keyboard into a file named FASTNOTE.TXT, you enter

```
copy con fastnote.txt
```

If you want to send what you type directly to the printer rather than to a file, you enter

```
copy con prn
```

In both cases, when you've finished typing, you need to press Ctrl-Z or F6 and then press Enter to terminate the COPY command.

More stuff

When sending output from one device to another device or to a file, be sure that you don't mess up and specify a device that you don't own (or mistype the name of a device you do actually have) because this mistake has been known to throw DOS for a loop that could crash your computer.

COPY (File to Device)

Copies a file to a device like your printer.

DOSspeak

COPY *source* [/a] [/b] *device*

Variable or Option	Function
source	Specifies the path and name of the file whose output you want to copy to the device.
/a	Indicates that the *source* file is an ASCII (text) file.

| /b | Indicates that the *source* file is a binary file. |
| *device* | Specifies the device to which the output of the *source* file is to be copied. |

Sample

To send a copy of a file named README.TXT to your printer, you enter

```
copy readme.txt prn
```

To send the same file to the screen, you enter

```
copy readme.txt con
```

See the example in *DOS For Dummies,* Chapter 3, section "Printing a Text File."

More stuff

When sending a file to a device, such as your printer or the screen, be aware that if you mistype the name of the device, the computer may freeze up on you, forcing you to reset it.

COPY *(File to File)*

Copies a file to another file or a group of files to another group of files.

DOSspeak

COPY *source destination* [/a] [/b] [/v]

Variable or Option	Function
source	Specifies the directory and name of the file(s) to be copied.
destination	Specifies the directory and/or name for the new files.
/a	Indicates that the *source* and/or *destination* files are ASCII (text) files.
/b	Indicates that the *source* and/or *destination* files are binary files.
/v	Verifies that the new *destination* files match the *source* files from which they are copied.

The /a and /b switches affect the filename that immediately precedes them in the command line as well any filenames that follow them — until DOS encounters another /a or /b switch.

Sample

Suppose that Al in Finance needs a copy of your worksheet, FORECAST.WK1, that's in the \123STUFF directory on your drive C. Currently, you're logged on to the root directory of drive C and have Al's floppy disk in drive A. To make a copy of the worksheet on his floppy disk, you enter

```
copy \123stuff\forcast.wk1 a:
```

Now, suppose that you're already logged on to your \123STUFF directory and you want to copy all your worksheets to a directory called \MYMESSES. This time, you need to enter

```
copy *.wk1 c:\mymesses
```

See the examples in *DOS For Dummies,* Chapter 3, sections "Duplicating a File," "Copying a Single File," "Copying a File to You," and "Copying a Group of Files."

More stuff

If the *source* and *destination* parameters indicate the same file in the same location on a disk, you'll get an error message indicating that DOS is completely faked out because the file cannot be copied onto itself.

Although COPY is usually a pretty "user-friendly" command, you can get yourself into trouble if you mistakenly specify an existing filename as the *destination* file whose data you don't really want replaced by the *source* file. Keep in mind that if the *destination* file exists, COPY replaces it with the *source* file information without asking you for any confirmation, and DOS provides *no way* to undo this type of boo-boo!

CTTY

Reroutes console input and output to a hardware device like the COM1 or COM2 communications port.

DOSspeak

CTTY *device*

where *device* is a valid hardware device name like COM1 or AUX.

Sample

To reroute the input and output through the COM1 communications port, you enter

```
ctty com1
```

To once again route input and output through keyboard and screen, you enter

```
ctty con
```

Note, however, that this latter command must be sent via the COM1 port — you can't just type it from the keyboard because the keyboard is no longer the computer's input device!

DATE

Displays or sets the date used by DOS and application programs to add the date stamp to files.

DOSspeak

DATE [*month-day-year*]

Variable or Option	Function
month	Specifies the *month* as a number between 1 and 12.
day	Specifies the *day* as a number between 1 and 31 (no need to include leading zeros, such as 01).
year	Specifies the *year* in the 20th century as a number between 80 and 99 (for dates in the 21st century, enter all four digits of the year, such as 2001).

You can type DATE without any parameters to display the current date setting.

Sample

To see what day your computer thinks it is, you enter

```
date
```

and press Enter at the `Enter new date (mm-dd-yy)` prompt. Suppose that today is really May Day, 1994, but DOS still thinks it's April Fool's day. To set the date straight, you type

```
date 5-1-94
```

and press Enter.

See the example in *DOS For Dummies,* Chapter 6, section "The Date and Time."

More stuff

Even though DOS doesn't tell you, it *will* accept a date separated with slashes instead of dashes — such as 2/15/94 instead of 2-15-94. Also, even though when you use the DATE command DOS *shows* you the day of the week preceding the date, DOS won't accept an entry of anything but the actual date. Finally, if someone's fooled around with the COUNTRY command, you may have to vary the date format to something like 15-2-94 (for February 15, 1994).

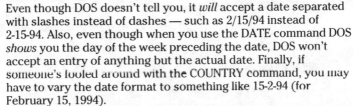

DBLSPACE (Check Disk)

Checks a compressed floppy or hard disk for errors, such as lost clusters or cross-linked files (available only in DOS 6).

DOSspeak

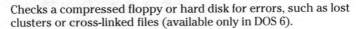

DBLSPACE `[/chkdsk]` `[/f]` `[drive:]`

Variable or Option	Function
/chkdsk	Instructs the DoubleSpace program to check the structural integrity of a compressed disk (you can abbreviate it to /chk).
/f	Fixes errors on the compressed disk.
drive:	Specifies the drive with the compressed disk you want checked. If you omit this parameter, DOS assumes you mean the current drive.

If you enter DBLSPACE without any parameters, DOS starts the DoubleSpace program, in which you can use menu options to check the compressed disk.

Sample

To check drive C after you've compressed it, you enter

```
dblspace /chkdsk c:
```

More Stuff

DOS 6.2 replaces this command with SCANDISK.

DBLSPACE (Compress)

Compresses a floppy or hard disk to free up more space (available only in DOS 6+).

DOSspeak

> **DBLSPACE** [/compress] *drive1:* [/newdrive=*drive2:*]
> [/reserve=*size*] [/f]

Variable or Option	Function
/compress	Tells DOS to compress the specified disk (you can abbreviate this switch to /com).
drive1:	Specifies the existing drive containing the disk you want to compress.
/newdrive=*drive2*	Specifies the drive letter for the uncompressed (host) drive. When DoubleSpace compresses an existing drive, your system includes both the existing (compressed) drive and a new (uncompressed) drive. If you omit the /newdrive switch, DoubleSpace assigns the next available drive letter (you can abbreviate the /newdrive switch to /new).
/reserve=*size*	Specifies how many megabytes of space to leave uncompressed for files like the Windows swap file that don't work correctly when compressed. The uncompressed space reserved with this switch resides on the new (uncompressed) drive (you can abbreviate this switch to /res).
/f	Suppresses the display of the final screen of statistics.

If you enter DBLSPACE alone, DOS starts the DoubleSpace program, in which you can use the menu options to compress your disk.

Sample

To compress your hard disk on drive C, make drive D the new (uncompressed) drive, and reserve 2 megabytes of uncompressed space on this new disk, you enter

```
dblspace /compress c: /new=d: /res=2
```

More stuff

To compress your startup hard disk, you must have at least 1.7M of space free. To compress other hard disks, you need at least 1M free. To compress floppy disks, you must have at least 200K free (you can't compress 360K floppies).

DBLSPACE *(Convert Stacker Volume)*

Converts a volume compressed with the Stacker compression utility to the DoubleSpace compression format (available only in DOS 6).

DOSspeak

DBLSPACE [/convstac=*stacvol*] [*drive1:*] [/newdrive=*drive2:*] [/cvf=*sss*]

Variable or Option	Function
/convstac=*stacvol*	Specifies the Stacker volume to convert. The volume specified by the *stacvol* parameter must be on the drive specified by the *drive1:* parameter (you can abbreviate this switch to /convst).
drive1:	Specifies the hard disk that contains the Stacker volume you want to convert.
/newdrive=*drive2:*	Specifies the drive letter for the newly converted compressed drive. If you omit the /newdrive switch, DoubleSpace assigns the next available drive letter (you can abbreviate this switch to /new).
/cvf=*sss*	Specifies the filename extension for the new compressed volume file. The *sss* parameter can be a number between 000 and 254. If you omit the /cvf switch, DoubleSpace assigns the next available extension, such as DBLSPACE.001.

If you enter DBLSPACE alone, DOS starts the DoubleSpace program, in which you can use the menu options to convert a Stacker volume to the DoubleSpace format.

DBLSPACE (Create)

Creates a new compressed drive by using free space on an uncompressed drive (available only in DOS 6+).

DOSspeak

```
DBLSPACE [/create] [drive1:] [/newdrive=drive2:]
[/size=size | /reserve=size]
```

Variable or Option	Function
/create	Creates the new compressed drive using the uncompressed drive specified by the *drive1:* parameter (you can abbreviate this switch to /c).
drive1:	Specifies the uncompressed drive whose space is to be used in creating the new compressed drive.
/newdrive=*drive2:*	Specifies the letter of the new compressed drive you are creating. If you omit the /newdrive switch, DOS assigns the next available drive (you can abbreviate this switch to /n).
/size=*size*	Specifies the amount of space (in megabytes) on the uncompressed drive that you want to allocate to the compressed drive (you can abbreviate this switch to /si). You can't use the /size switch with the /reserve switch (see next option).
/reserve=*size*	Specifies how much free space (in megabytes) DoubleSpace should leave on the uncompressed drive. To make the compressed drive as big as possible, specify 0 as the *size* parameter (you can abbreviate this switch to /re). You can't use the /reserve switch with the /size switch. If you omit both switches, DoubleSpace reserves 1M of free space. In Version 6.2, the new default for this switch is 2M.

If you enter DBLSPACE alone, DOS starts the DoubleSpace program, in which you can use the menu options to create a new compressed disk.

DBLSPACE (Defragment)

Defragments a compressed disk by consolidating its free space (available only in DOS 6+).

DOSspeak

```
DBLSPACE [/defragment] [drive:] [/f]
```

Variable or Option	Function
/defragment	Tells the DoubleSpace program to consolidate all free space on the compressed disk specified by the *drive:* parameter (you can abbreviate this switch to /def).
drive:	Specifies the compressed disk to defragment.
/f	Enables the drive to be defragmented more fully.

If you enter DBLSPACE alone, DOS starts the DoubleSpace program, in which you can use the menu options to defragment a compressed disk.

Sample

To defragment your compressed hard disk (drive C), you enter

```
dblspace /def c:
```

More stuff

If you intend to further compress a compressed drive — see DBLSPACE (Maxcompress) — you should first consolidate the free space with the DBLSPACE /DEFRAGMENT command.

DBLSPACE (Delete)

Deletes a compressed drive and all the files on it (available only in DOS 6+).

DOSspeak

```
DBLSPACE [/delete] [drive:]
```

Variable or Option	Function
/delete	Tells the DoubleSpace program to delete all the files on the compressed disk specified by the *drive:* parameter (you can abbreviate this switch to /del).
drive:	Specifies the compressed disk to delete (DoubleSpace won't let you delete drive C, however).

If you enter DBLSPACE alone, DOS starts the DoubleSpace program, in which you can use the menu options to delete a compressed disk.

More stuff

If you delete a compressed disk by mistake, you may be able to restore it. First, use the UNDELETE command to restore the deleted compressed volume file (using a filename like DBLSPACE.*xxx,* such as DBLSPACE.001). After undeleting this file, use the DBLSPACE /MOUNT command to mount the file again — see DBLSPACE (Mount).

DBLSPACE (DoubleGuard)

Enables or disables DoubleGuard. Enabled, DoubleSpace checks its memory looking for damage from another program and preventing lots of data loss by stopping the computer when it finds damage. Note that you have to restart your computer to make this switch work.

DOSspeak

```
DBLSPACE [/doubleguard=0 | 1]
```

Variable or Option	Function
0	Keeps DoubleSpace from looking for damage in its memory.
1	Tells DoubleSpace to look for damage in its memory.

DBLSPACE (Format)

Formats a compressed disk (available only in DOS 6+).

DOSspeak

```
DBLSPACE [/format] [drive:]
```

Variable or Option **Function**

/format   Tells the DoubleSpace program to format the
                 compressed disk specified by the *drive:*
                 parameter (you can abbreviate this switch to /f).

drive: Specifies the compressed disk to format.

If you enter DBLSPACE alone, DOS starts the DoubleSpace
program, in which you can use the menu options to format a
compressed disk.

More stuff

Be careful. You completely delete all the drive's compressed data
just as the standard FORMAT wipes out all existing data on an
uncompressed drive when you format a compressed disk with
the DBLSPACE /FORMAT command.

DBLSPACE (Info)

Displays lots of useful information about a compressed drive,
including the drive's used and free space, the name of its compressed
volume, and its compression ratios (available only in DOS 6+).

DOSspeak

```
DBLSPACE [/info] [drive:]
```

Variable or Option **Function**

/info   Tells the DoubleSpace program to give you
                 information on the compressed disk specified
                 by the *drive:* parameter. You can omit this
                 switch altogether as long as you specify the
                 drive: parameter.

drive: Specifies the compressed disk you want
                 information on.

If you enter DBLSPACE alone, DOS starts the DoubleSpace
program, in which you can use the menu options to get information about a compressed disk.

Sample

To get information on your compressed hard disk (drive C), you
enter

```
dblspace /info c:
```

You can also enter this command simply as

```
dblspace c:
```

✓ DBLSPACE (List)

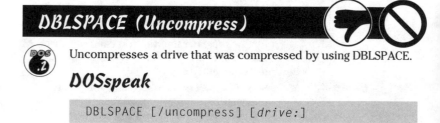

Lists all your computer's drives (except for network drives) with
a brief description (available only in DOS 6).

DOSspeak

```
DBLSPACE [/list]
```

where /list tells DoubleSpace to display a listing of local (non-
network) drives on your computer (you may abbreviate this
switch to /l). If you enter DBLSPACE alone, DOS starts the
DoubleSpace program, in which you can use the menu options to
list your local drives.

Sample

To get a list of all the compressed and uncompressed local drives
on your computer, you enter

```
dblspace /list
```

DBLSPACE (Uncompress)

Uncompresses a drive that was compressed by using DBLSPACE.

DOSspeak

```
DBLSPACE [/uncompress] [drive:]
```

Variable or Option	Function
/uncompress	Tells DOS to uncompress the specified disk.
drive:	Specifies the letter of the compressed drive.

DBLSPACE (Mount)

Establishes a connection between a compressed volume file (CVF) and a drive letter so that you can use the files in this compressed volume file. You only have to mount a CVF when you've previously unmounted it with the DBLSPACE /unmount switch or when the CVF is on a floppy disk (available only in DOS 6+).

DOSspeak

DBLSPACE [/mount[=*nnn*]] [*drive1:*] [/newdrive=*drive2:*]

Variable or Option	Function
/mount[=*nnn*]	Mounts the compressed volume file with the extension specified by the *nnn* parameter. If you omit the *nnn* parameter, DoubleSpace mounts the CVF named DBLSPACE.000 (you can enter the /mount switch as /mo).
drive1:	Specifies the drive that contains the compressed volume file (CVF) that you want to mount. You must supply this parameter when using the /mount switch.
/newdrive=*drive2:*	Specifies the drive letter you want assigned to the newly mounted CVF. If you omit this parameter, DoubleSpace uses the next available drive letter (you can abbreviate this switch to /new).

If you enter DBLSPACE alone, DOS starts the DoubleSpace program, in which you can use menu options to mount a compressed volume file.

Sample

To mount a compressed floppy disk in drive A, you enter

```
dblspace /mount a:
```

DBLSPACE (Unmount)

Breaks a connection between a compressed volume file (CVF) and a drive letter, making the CVF files temporarily unusable (available only in DOS 6+).

DOSspeak

```
DBLSPACE [/unmount] [drive:]
```

Variable or Option	Function
/unmount	Unmounts the compressed drive specified by the *drive:* parameter (you can abbreviate this switch to /u).
drive:	Specifies the letter of the compressed drive to unmount. If you omit this parameter, DoubleSpace unmounts the current drive.

If you enter DBLSPACE alone, DOS starts the DoubleSpace program, in which you can use menu options to unmount a compressed drive.

Sample

To unmount compressed drive A, you enter

```
dblspace /unmount a:
```

DBLSPACE (Ratio)

Modifies the compression ratio that estimates how much free space is available on a compressed drive (available only in DOS 6+).

DOSspeak

```
DBLSPACE /ratio[=r.r] [drive: | /all]
xcopy c:\myturf\*.* a: /s /d:02/15/93
```

Variable or Option	Function
/ratio[=*r.r*]	Changes the estimated compression ratio for the compressed drive specified by the *drive:* or all parameters to the ratio specified by the *r.r* parameter (between 1.0 and 16.0). If you omit the *r.r* parameter, DoubleSpace sets the drive's estimated compression ratio to the actual average ratio for all the files on the specified drive (you can abbreviate this switch to /ra).
drive:	Specifies the letter of the compressed drive whose estimated compression ratio is to be tweaked. If you don't use this parameter or the /all switch (see below), DoubleSpace changes the ratio for the current drive.
/all	Changes the estimated compression ratio for all the mounted compressed drives. You can't use this switch with the *drive:* parameter.

If you enter DBLSPACE alone, DOS starts the DoubleSpace program, in which you can use menu options to change the compression ratio for a compressed drive.

Sample

To increase the drive C estimated compression ratio to 8 to 1, you enter

```
dblspace /ratio=8 c:
```

More stuff

Each time you start your computer, DoubleSpace adjusts the estimated compression ratio to match the average compression ratio of the files currently stored on that compressed drive.

DBLSPACE (Size)

Changes the size of a compressed drive (available only in DOS 6+).

DOSspeak

```
DBLSPACE [/size[=size1 | /reserve=size2]] [drive:]
```

Variable or Option	Function
/size=*size1*	Changes the size of the compressed drive specified by the *drive:* parameter to the size specified by the *size1* parameter. The *size1* parameter is the number of megabytes of space which that drive's compressed volume file takes on the uncompressed (host) drive (you can abbreviate the /size switch to /si). You can specify the new size with either the /size or /reserve switch (see the following option) but not with both. If you omit both switches, DoubleSpace makes the specified drive as small as possible.
/reserve=*size2*	Specifies the free space (in megabytes) that you want the uncompressed (host) drive to retain after DoubleSpace resizes the drive specified by the *drive:* parameter (you can abbreviate this switch to /res).
drive:	Specifies the compressed drive that you want to resize. You must specify a drive when you use the /size switch.

If you enter DBLSPACE alone, DOS starts the DoubleSpace program, in which you can use menu options to change the size of a compressed drive.

Sample

To resize your compressed drive C so that it's as large as possible, you enter

```
dblspace /size /reserve=0 c:
```

DEFRAG

Reorganizes the files on a disk to optimize disk performance (available only in DOS 6+).

DOSspeak

```
DEFRAG [drive:] [/f] [/s[:]order] [/b]
[skiphigh] [lcd | /bw | /go] [/h]
```

or

```
DEFRAG [drive:] [/u] [/b] [/skiphigh]
[lcd | /bw | /go] [/h]
```

Variable or Option	Function
drive:	Specifies the drive with the disk you want to optimize.
/f	Ensures that there are no empty spaces between files when defragmenting a disk.
/u	Leaves the empty spaces between files when defragmenting a disk.
/s[:]*order*	Sorts files in their directories according to the *order* parameter when defragmenting a disk. The order parameter can be any of the following values: n (for alphabetic order by filename), n- (for reverse alphabetic order by name), e (for alphabetic order by extension), e- (for reverse alphabetic order by extension), d (for date and time order, least recent to most recent), d- (for date and time order, most recent to least recent), s (for size order, smallest to largest), or s- (for size order, largest to smallest). When combining *order* parameters, don't separate them with spaces.
/b	Reboots your computer as soon as DEFRAG finishes optimizing your drive.
/skiphigh	Loads DEFRAG into conventional memory rather than upper memory (as is usually the case when sufficient upper memory is available).
/lcd	Displays the DEFRAG screen in an LCD color scheme.
/bw	Displays the DEFRAG screen in a black-and-white color scheme.
/go	Disables the graphics character set and the graphical mouse pointer in the DEFRAG screen.
/h	Moves hidden files when defragmenting a disk.

If you enter DEFRAG without any parameters, DOS loads DEFRAG and displays the DEFRAG screen using the default display values.

Sample

To optimize drive C and sort the files in date-and-time order, most recent to least recent, you enter

```
defrag c: /f /sd-
```

More stuff

You can't use the DEFRAG command when you are running Microsoft Windows, nor can you use it to optimize network drives (or drives connected with the INTERLNK command). Also, be aware that optimizing a large hard disk is a time-consuming process. Therefore, you may want to enter the DEFRAG command right before you leave the office so that DEFRAG can optimize your disk overnight.

DEL or ERASE

Deletes one or more files from your disk.

DOSspeak

> **DEL** [*drive:*][*path*]*filename* [/p]

or

> **ERASE** [*drive:*][*path*]*filename* [/p]

Variable or Option	Function
[*drive:*][*path*]*filename*	Specifies the drive, directory, and names of the file(s) to be erased. If the *drive:* and/or *path* parameters are omitted, DOS assumes that you want to use the current drive and directory. Use wildcard characters to delete a group of files. Beware of the *.* wildcard combination because, used with this command, it will erase all files in the current directory.
/p	(Versions 4+) Specifies that DOS will prompt you before deleting each file.

Sample

To delete the file named GARBAGE.DOC in your C:\MYJUNK
directory when the root directory on drive C is current, you enter

```
del \myjunk\garbage.doc
```

To delete all the files in your \MYJUNK directory that use the file
extension CRP when the \MYJUNK directory is current, you enter

```
erase *.crp
```

See the examples in *DOS For Dummies,* Chapter 3, sections
"Deleting a File" and "Deleting a Group of Files."

More stuff

The DEL and ERASE commands are identical in purpose (obviously they differ in name). Also, if you like to do more typing, you
can type DELETE instead of DEL when erasing files.

Unless you are using DOS Version 5 or later or have a fancy DOS
utility that can bring deleted files back from the dead, all dele-
tions made with ERASE or DEL are final. Therefore, *before* you
enter this command, be sure that

1. You're in the right directory — see DIR.

2. You've typed the right path and filename(s).

3. You've got the files backed up on another disk (unless
   they're just complete garbage) — see BACKUP and COPY.

DELTREE

Deletes a directory and all the files and subdirectories in it
(available only in DOS 6+).

DOSspeak

DELTREE [/y] [*drive:*]***path***

Variable or Option	Function
/y	Deletes all the files and subdirectories in the specified directory without prompting you for confirmation (a potentially danger- ous switch).
[*drive:*]*path*	Specifies the drive and directory whose files and subdirectories are to be deleted.

Sample

To delete all the files and subdirectories in your \MYJUNK
directory (including the two subdirectories \HOTTRASH and
\RUBBISH), you enter

```
deltree c:\myjunk
```

More stuff

Be careful with the DELTREE command because it deletes *all* files
in the specified directory or subdirectories regardless of their
attributes — including files marked with the read-only, hidden,
and system attributes.

DIR

Displays a list of all the files and subdirectories in a directory.

```
DIR [drive:][path][filename] [/p] [/w]
[/a[[:]attributes]] [/o[[:]sortorder]] [/s]
[/b] [/l] [/c[h]]
```

Variable or Option	Function
[*drive:*][*path*][*filename*]	Specifies the drive, directories, or files to include in the directory listing.
/p	Pauses the directory listing after each screenful of information and displays the message Press any key to continue.
/w	Displays the directory listing in a wide format in five columns across the screen. In the wide format in Versions 5+, the names of subdirectories are enclosed in square brackets, such as [MYTURF].
/a:*attributes*	(Versions 5+) Restricts the directory listing to just those entries with the particular attribute parameter.
	Attribute parameters include a for Archive, d for Directory, h for Hidden, r for Read-only, and s for System files.
	To exclude particular attributes from a directory listing, preface the *attribute* parameter with a dash (hyphen), such

as `dir /a:-s` to eliminate all system files from the directory listing.

If you use the /a switch without any *attribute* parameter, DOS displays all entries, including hidden and system files.

/o:*sortorder*   (Versions 5+) Specifies the sort order in which entries are displayed in the directory listing (see *More stuff*).

Sortorder parameters include n for alphabetical order by filename, e for alphabetical order by extension, s for ascending order by size (smallest to largest), d for ascending order by date and time (oldest to newest), or g to place subdirectories ahead of files in the list.

To reverse the sort order (display the files in order of largest to smallest), preface the *sortorder* parameter with a dash (hyphen), such as `dir /o:-s`.

If you use the /o switch without any *sortorder* parameter, DOS sorts the entries by name and places subdirectories ahead of files.

/s   (Versions 5+) Displays files in the directory specified by the *path* parameter *and* the files in all its subdirectories.

/b   (Versions 5+) Displays the directory listing in a bare-bones format, without the size and revision date and time information or the summary information.

/l   (Versions 5+) Displays all file and subdirectory names in lowercase letters.

/c[h]   (Version 6) Displays the compression ratio of files compressed with DoubleSpace, based on an 8K cluster size. The optional h parameter displays the compression ratio based on the cluster size of the host drive. The h parameter is ignored when used with the /w or /b switch.

If you enter DIR without any parameters, DOS lists all files and subdirectories of the current directory in one blur.

Sample

Let's suppose that you're in your \MYTURF directory and you want a wide listing of all the files without listing any of the subdirectories like \MYMESSES. You enter

```
dir /w /a:-d
```

Now, you decide you want to see all the files in this directory in descending order of their revision date and time (newest to oldest). Because you have so much junk in this directory, you also want DOS to pause at each screenful. To do so, you enter

```
dir /p /o:-d
```

See the examples in *DOS For Dummies,* Chapter 17, sections "Using the DIR Command," "The wide DIR command," "Making DIR display one screen at a time," and "Displaying a sorted directory."

DISKCOMP

Compares the contents of two floppy disks track by track and, if the disks are not identical, reports on which tracks are different.

DOSspeak

DISKCOMP [*drive1:* [*drive2:*]] [/1] [/8]

Variable or Option	Function
drive1:	Specifies the drive containing the first floppy disk to be compared.
drive2:	Specifies the drive containing the second floppy disk to be compared.
/1	Restricts the disk comparison to just the first side of the floppy disks even when the disks are double-sided.
/8	Limits the disk comparison to the first 8 sectors per track even if the first floppy disk has 9 or even 15 sectors per track.

If you omit the *drive2:* parameter, DOS compares the floppy disk specified with *drive1:* to the disk in the current floppy drive (make sure that you're not logged on to the hard drive). If you omit both drive parameters, DOS assumes that you want to use *only* the current floppy drive when comparing disks (useful if you only have a drive A) and prompts you to insert the different disks.

Sample

Suppose that you've got nothing better to do, and you're dying to verify that the copy of the floppy disk you just made with DISKCOPY for Al in Finance is identical to your original floppy disk. To do so, you make drive A current by typing

```
a:
```

and pressing Enter. Then you enter

```
diskcomp
```

Next, in response to the prompt Insert FIRST diskette in drive A:, you put the original floppy disk in drive A, and press Enter. When prompted by DOS with Insert SECOND diskette in drive A:, you replace the original disk with Al's copy in drive A and press Enter. Then you press N when DOS asks if you want to compare another disk (you do have *useful* work to do, don't you?).

More stuff

You can't use DISKCOMP to compare disks of different types, such as a double-sided 360K disk with a high-density 1.2M disk. Also, don't try using DISKCOMP with a drive under the influence of the JOIN or ASSIGN commands (but, then again, why are using DISKCOMP at all?).

DISKCOPY

Duplicates one floppy disk on another floppy disk of the same type.

DOSspeak

DISKCOPY [*drive1:* [*drive2:*]] [/l] [/v] [/m]

Variable or Option	Function
drive1:	Specifies the drive containing the floppy disk to be copied.
drive2:	Specifies the drive containing the floppy disk where the duplicate is to be made.
/l	Duplicates only the first side of the floppy disk in *drive1:* even when the disk is double-sided.

| /v | | (Versions 5+) Verifies that the duplicates are identical (making aforementioned DISKCOMP command superfluous). |

| /m | | Forces DISKCOPY to use only conventional memory for an interim storage area when copying one floppy to another. (DOS 6.2 uses the hard drive as an interim storage area.) |

If you omit the *drive2:* parameter, DOS copies the floppy disk specified with *drive1:* onto the disk in the current floppy drive (make sure that you're not logged on to the hard disk). If you omit both drive parameters, DOS assumes that you want to use *only* the current floppy drive when duplicating disks (useful if you only have a drive A) and prompts you to insert the different disks.

Sample

Suppose that you need to make a duplicate of a floppy disk for Al in Finance. You put your original floppy disk in drive A and an unformatted floppy disk in drive B; then you enter

```
diskcopy a: b: /v
```

Now, suppose that today you're working on Sue's machine and her old klunker has only one floppy drive. To make another copy of your floppy disk for Al, this time you put your original in Sue's floppy drive, type

```
a:
```

and press Enter to log on to drive A; then type

```
diskcopy
```

Press Enter at the prompt `Insert SOURCE diskette in drive A:` to start the copy process and then replace the original floppy disk with the new unformatted floppy disk when you see the `Insert TARGET diskette in drive A:` prompt. Press Enter to start the copy. You follow the prompts, switching to the original disk when prompted for the `SOURCE diskette` and to the duplicate disk when prompted for the `TARGET diskette`.

See the example in *DOS For Dummies,* Chapter 12, section "Duplicating Disks (the DISKCOPY Command)."

More stuff

You can't use DISKCOPY to copy a disk of a different type — for example, a double-sided 360K disk onto a high-density 1.2M disk.

DOSHELP

Displays an alphabetical list of all DOS and batch commands or a short description of a particular command (including the DOSspeak line and a listing of the parameters).

DOSspeak

DOSHELP [*command*]

where *command* is the name of the DOS command you want help information on. If you enter DOSHELP without entering a command, DOS displays a quick list of all the DOS 6 commands.

Sample

Al in Finance has borrowed your copy of the *DOS For Dummies Quick Reference* and you need information right now on how to back up all the files in your \MYTURF directory that have been modified since last December. To display help on the BACKUP command in the hope that you get these backups made before next December, you enter

```
doshelp backup
```

DOSKEY

Installs a DOSKEY utility that lets you recall previously used DOS commands to the command line, edit DOS commands on the command line with the ← and → before you enter them, and create macros that play back DOS commands (DOSKEY is available in Versions 5+ only).

DOSspeak

DOSKEY [/reinstall] [/bufsize=*size*] [/macros]
[/history] [/insert] [/overstrike]
[*macroname*=⌊*text*⌋]

Variable or Option	Function
/resinstall	Installs a new copy of DOSKEY into memory, wiping out any commands or macros currently in memory.

/bufsize=*size*	Specifies the *size* in bytes of the area in memory (called a *buffer*) where DOSKEY stores your commands and macros (the default is 512 bytes). You can use this switch only when you first start or reinstall DOSKEY.
/macros	Displays all DOSKEY macros currently in the DOSKEY buffer.
/history	Displays all DOS commands currently in the DOSKEY buffer.
/insert	Puts DOSKEY in Insert mode so that new characters are inserted into the old text.
/overstrike	Puts DOSKEY in Overtype mode so that new characters replace old text (this is the default).
macroname	Specifies the name for a macro that you want to record.
text	Specifies the DOS commands that you want to record in your macro.

Sample

To install DOSKEY so that you can edit DOS commands with the arrow keys as well as recall previously used commands to the command line with the arrow keys, you enter

```
doskey
```

After installing DOSKEY, you can use the ↑ and ↓ keys to move up and down through the DOS commands you've used since you started DOSKEY. To edit a DOS command, use the ← and → keys to move the cursor to the characters that need editing. To display a numbered list of all the DOS commands in memory, press F7. To select a command by number, press F9 and then enter its number. To clear the DOSKEY buffer of all DOS commands, press Alt-F7.

DOSSHELL

Starts the DOS shell, a menu-driven utility that enables you to perform many basic DOS tasks without ever having to type a single one of these awful DOS commands (sorry folks, this utility is available only for Versions 4+).

DOSspeak

DOSSHELL [/t[:res[*n*]]] [/b]

or

DOSSHELL [/g[:res[*n*]]] [/b]	

Variable or Option	**Function**
/t	Starts the DOS shell in text mode.
/g	Starts the DOS shell in graphics mode.
:res[*n*]	Specifies the screen resolution that the DOS shell is to use. The *n* parameters include l for low resolution, m for medium, and h for high resolution.
/b	Forces the DOS shell to be displayed in monochrome on a color monitor (use this switch to increase the screen contrast on a laptop that normally uses shades of gray to represent colors).

Sample

To start the DOS shell program from the DOS prompt, you type

```
dosshell
```

When you've finished having fun in the DOS shell and are ready to get back to reality at the DOS prompt, press Alt-F4 or Alt-FX to quit the DOS shell.

For loads of good information on how to use the DOS shell, see Chapter 4, "Easier DOS: The DOS Shell," in *DOS For Dummies*.

EDIT

Starts the DOS Editor that you can use to edit text files, such as those weird AUTOEXEC.BAT and CONFIG.SYS files that application programs are always trying to get you to edit.

DOSspeak

EDIT [[*drive:*][*path*]*filename*] [/b] [/g] [/h] [/nohi]	

Variable or Option	**Function**
[*drive:*][*path*]*filename*	Specifies the drive, directory, and name of a new or existing file that you want to edit.

/b	Forces the Editor to appear in mono-chrome on a color monitor (use this switch to increase the screen contrast on a laptop that normally uses shades of gray to represent colors).
/g	Provides the fastest possible screen response when using the Editor with CGA graphics (the old standard Color/Graphics adapter).
/h	Displays the maximum number of lines possible on your monitor.
/nohi	Suppresses the display of high-intensity video while using the Editor. (Don't use this switch on laptops because it routinely crashes them.)

Sample

Let's suppose that there's no way around it (Al in Finance is on vacation in Tahiti for the rest of the month). You have to bite the bullet and edit the AUTOEXEC.BAT file on your computer *all by yourself!* To start the DOS Editor and load this file, you enter

```
edit c:\autoexec.bat
```

After (carefully) making and checking over your changes to this crucial file, press Alt-FX and then press Y when asked if you want to save your changes.

See the example in *DOS For Dummies,* Chapter 15, section "Using the DOS Editor."

 EDLIN

Starts that truly dreadful EDLIN Editor that you can use to edit text files (if absolutely nothing else is available and your boss refuses to upgrade to the latest version of DOS — however, if you get the boss to upgrade, see EDIT above and forget the rest of this entry).

DOSspeak

EDLIN [*drive:*][*path*]*filename*] [/b]

Variable or Option	Function
[drive:][path]filename	Specifies the drive, directory, and name of a new or existing file that you want to edit with EDLIN.
/b	Causes EDLIN to ignore all Ctrl-Z characters (those end-of-line thingies) in the file.

Sample

I just haven't got the heart to give you an example of using this monstrosity, so please see *DOS For Dummies,* Chapter 15, section "Using EDLIN" if there's no way to persuade you to use something else!

EXE2BIN

Converts an executable file (that is, a file with an EXE extension) to a binary-image format (that is, a file with a BIN extension) — and who said DOS commands were hard to understand?

DOSspeak

EXE2BIN *[drive1:][path1]input–file*
[[drive2:][path2]output–file]

Variable or Option	Function
[drive1:][path1]input–file	Specifies the drive, path, and name of the executable file (with the EXE extension) to be converted to the binary format.
[drive2:][path2]output–file	Specifies the drive, path, and name of the binary format file to be created from the *input–file*. If no *output–file* is specified, DOS names it with the same filename as that of the *input–file* and adds a BIN extension to the main filename.

Sample

Let's suppose (for argument's sake, at least) that you've just finished creating your first executable file, called EXILEDOS.EXE, and now you want to convert it to a binary format. To do so, you enter

```
exe2bin exiledos
```

and DOS converts EXILEDOS.EXE to EXILEDOS.BIN.

More stuff

This DOS command (as if you couldn't guess) is for advanced programmers, preferably those with Assembly language experience — all others need not apply!

EXIT

Returns control from a second copy of the command interpreter (started with the COMMAND command) to the parent command interpreter.

DOSspeak

EXIT

Sample

Suppose that you're working away in Lotus 1-2-3. When you decide to save a file, instead of typing /fs as you normally do, you mess up and type /s. You find yourself facing a blank screen with the DOS prompt where 1-2-3 and your worksheet should be (/s is 1-2-3's way of starting a second DOS command interpreter). To get back home to your 1-2-3 worksheet, you type

```
exit
```

at the DOS prompt; then press Enter to quit the second command interpreter and return immediately to 1-2-3 and your still unsaved worksheet.

See the example in *DOS For Dummies,* Chapter 19, section "How Do I Get Back?"

More stuff

See COMMAND earlier in this DOS Commands section for information on how to start the trouble that the EXIT command will get you out of.

EXPAND

Expands one or more compressed files (available in Versions 5+).

DOSspeak

EXPAND [*drive:*][*path*]***filename***
[[*drive1*][*path1*]*filename*[...]] *destination*

Variable or Option	Function
[*drive:*][*path*]*filename*	Specifies the drive, path, and name of the file or files that you want to expand. Note that you can't use wildcards in the *filename* parameter. To expand multiple files, you must list all the filenames separated by spaces.
destination	Specifies the new location and/or filename of the expanded file. If you are expanding multiple files, the *destination* parameter must consist solely of a *drive:* and/or *path* parameter without a *filename* parameter.

Sample

Al in Finance has given you a floppy disk with two compressed files called MEGAFILE.WK1 and MAMMOTH.DOC. To copy and expand these files in the \MYTURF directory on your hard disk, you put the floppy disk in drive A. At the C> prompt, you enter

```
expand a:megafile.wk1 a:mammoth.doc c:\myturf
```

FASTHELP

Displays a list of all DOS 6 commands with a brief explanation of each (available only in DOS 6+).

DOSspeak

FASTHELP [*command*]

where c*ommand* is the DOS command you want help on. If you enter FASTHELP without the *command* parameter, DOS displays an alphabetical list of all Version 6 commands.

Sample

You've forgotten how you use the MORE command to display just a screenful of info at a time. To get fast help on this command, you enter

```
fasthelp more
```

You could also get fast help by entering

```
more /?
```

at the DOS prompt.

FASTOPEN

Decreases the amount of time needed to open frequently used files and directories on the hard disk by storing their locations in a special part of memory called the filename cache.

DOSspeak

FASTOPEN *drive:*[[=]*n*] [*drive:*[[=]*n*] [...] [/x]

Variable or Option	Function
drive:	Specifies the hard drive(s) whose files and directories you want FASTOPEN to remember. In versions prior to 5, you can specify up to 4 hard drives. In Versions 5+, you can specify up to 24 hard drives.
n	Specifies the maximum number of file locations that FASTOPEN retains in its filename cache (48 is the default on each *drive:*). The *n* parameter can be a number between 10 and 999. When specifying multiple drives, the total of all locations can't exceed 999.
	In Versions 4+, you can include a second number (between 1 and 999) in the *n* parameter. The second number specifies the number of buffers that can hold the location of fragmented parts of files on each drive (the so-called file-extent entries). When specifying these buffers, you need to enclose the *n* parameter in parentheses and enter its number after the file locations, separated by a comma, for example, (100,20) where 100 is the number of file locations and 20 is the number of file-extent entries.

|/x | (Versions 4+) Specifies that FASTOPEN store the file locations in expanded memory (which must conform to the LIM 4.0 specification). |

You can use FASTOPEN only once per work session. To change the FASTOPEN settings, you must reset your computer. Note that DOS uses about 48K of RAM memory for each file location that it stores. Each time you open a file, DOS adds the name and location to the filename cache. When the cache is full, DOS removes the last-accessed file from the list to make room for the new file.

Sample

Let's suppose that something possesses you to use FASTOPEN on your hard disk. To do this really strange thing, you enter

```
fastopen c:
```

More stuff

Although, FASTOPEN can boost performance in some limited situations, it's also true that this command requires a great deal of memory to hold the locations of the files in the filename cache. Be careful that you don't find yourself creating a state of affairs where you not only don't get better performance but actually have trouble running some of your more memory-intensive applications.

You can't use FASTOPEN on a drive under the influence of the ASSIGN, JOIN, or SUBST commands, nor can you use it on a network drive.

FC

Compares two files or sets of files and reports back on any differences between them.

DOSspeak

FC [/a] [/c] [/l] [/lb*n*] [/n] [/t] [/w] [/*nnnn*]
[*drive1:*][*path1*]***filename1*** [*drive2:*][*path2*]***filename2***

or

FC [/b] [*drive1:*][*path1*]***filename1***
[*drive2:*][*path2*]***filename2***

Variable or Option	Function
[*drive1:*][*path1*]*filename1*	Specifies the drive, path, and name of the first file or set of files you want to compare.
[*drive2:*][*path2*]*filename2*	Specifies the drive, path, and name of the second file or set of files you want to compare.
/a	Shortens the report by displaying only the first and last lines for each set of differences.
/b	Performs a binary comparison in which DOS compares the files byte by byte and reports the offset location of all differences. When using the /b switch, all other switches except the */nnnn* switch are off limits.
/c	Ignores case differences when comparing text (ASCII) files (DOS treats the text as though it were entered in all uppercase letters).
/l	Forces DOS to perform a line-by-line comparison of the files as though they were ASCII files (the default, except when the file extension is EXE, COM, SYS, OBJ, LIB, or BIN).
/lb*n*	Sets the maximum number of consecutive mismatches in the difference report to the number of lines specified by the *n* parameter (the default is 100 lines).
/n	Displays lines numbers when performing an ASCII comparison.
/t	Causes DOS to compare the tabs in the files literally — when the /t switch isn't used, DOS expands tabs to eight spaces.
/w	Causes DOS to ignore leading and trailing spaces and tabs in the files and to compress consecutive tabs and spaces in a line down to a single space.

/nnnn	Specifies the number of consecutive lines (or bytes in a binary comparison) that must match after DOS finds a mismatch. If a number less than the number entered as the *nnnn* parameter is found, DOS includes the match in the difference report (the default is 2).

Sample

Suppose that while doing a directory listing of your \MYTURF directory, you find two word processing files that you're pretty sure contain the same stuff even though they have different names (LETTER.DOC and EPISTLE.TXT). Do an ASCII file comparison to find out if they're the same by entering

```
fc letter.doc epistle.txt
```

Next, you switch to your \123STUFF directory where you notice two worksheets (BIGBUCKS.WK1 and LOTLUCRE.WK1) that you think might be duplicates. To do a binary file comparison to find out, you enter

```
fc /b bigbucks.wk1 lotlucre.wk1
```

FIND

Searches for a string of characters in a file or set of files.

DOSspeak

FIND [/v] [/c] [/n] [/i] *"string"*
[[*drive:*][*path*]*filename*[...]]

Variable or Option	Function
/v	Displays all lines that do NOT contain the *string*. If you use this switch with the /c switch, DOS will report the total number of lines that don't contain the *string*.
/c	Displays only the total number of lines that contain the *string*.
/n	Displays the line numbers along with the lines that contain the *string*.

/i	(Versions 5+) Ignores the case of the characters when searching for the *string*.
"*string*"	Specifies the string of characters to search for. The *string* parameter must be enclosed in a closed pair of quotation marks and is case sensitive unless you use the /i switch in the FIND command.
[*drive:*][*path*]*filename*	Specifies the drive, directory, and name of the file to be searched. To have DOS search multiple files, list each filename, separated by a space. If you omit this parameter, DOS searches your keyboard input until you press Ctrl-Z or F6 to terminate the input.

Sample

Suppose that you want to know how many lines in your work-for-hire contract called INDENTUR.DOC contain the phrase *grovel at my feet* (it's been one of those weeks!). To do so, you enter

```
find "grovel at my feet" indentur.doc /c
```

See the example in *DOS For Dummies,* Chapter 17, section "Finding a Lost Subdirectory."

FORMAT

Prepares a new disk so that DOS can store files on it. Keep in mind, however, that FORMAT is lethal to disks that already contain files because it wipes their little data banks totally clean!

DOSspeak

```
FORMAT drive: [/v[:label]] [/q]
[/u] [/f:size] [/b] [/s] [c]
```

or

```
FORMAT drive: [/v[:label]] [/q]
[/u] [/t:tracks /n:sectors] [/b] [/s] [c]
```

or

```
FORMAT drive: [/v[:label]] [/q]
[/u] [/1] [/4] [/8] [/b] [/s] [c]
```

Variable or Option	Function
drive:	Specifies the letter of the drive that contains the disk you want formatted. Unless you really intend to wipe out all the data on your *hard disk,* you will want to restrict this *drive:* parameter to only A or B, the designation for your first and second floppy disk drives, respectively.
/v[:*label*]	In versions before 4, indicates that you want to assign a volume label to the disk (versions after 4 automatically prompt you to enter a volume label when you format the disk). In Versions 4+, you can avoid the label prompt by specifying a *label* parameter with the /v switch that contains the text of the volume label (up to 11 characters) following a colon.
/q	(Versions 5+) Performs a quick format of a previously formatted disk.
/u	(Versions 5+) Performs an unconditional format that destroys all previous data on the disk — data that cannot later be restored with the UNFORMAT command. (This type of formatting is what versions of DOS before 5.0 perform.)
/f:*size*	(Versions 4+) Specifies the size of the disk to format. *Size* parameters can include 160 for a 160K disk, 180 for 180K, 320 for 320K, 360 for 360K, 720 for 720K, 1.2 for 1.2M, 1.44 for 1.44M, and 2.88 (Versions 5+) for 2.88M. Don't use this switch with the /1, /8, /t, or /n switches.
/b	Formats the disk to use only eight sectors per track (even when formatting a disk with 9 or 15 sectors) and leaves space for the DOS system files (without copying them on the disk — use SYS to do this part). You can't use this switch with /t or /s switches.
/s	Copies the system files to the formatted disk so that you can boot from that disk.
/c	Instructs the FORMAT command to retest bad clusters. (This was the default in previous versions of DOS.)
/t:*tracks*	(Version 3.3 only) Specifies the number of *tracks* on the formatted disk.
/n:*sectors*	(Version 3.3 only) Specifies the number of *sectors* per track on the formatted disk.

/1	Formats only one side of a floppy disk.
/4	(Versions 3.2+) Formats a double-density (360K) disk in a high-density (1.2M) drive.
/8	Formats eight sectors per track on 5¼" floppy disks instead of the normal 9 for double-sided or 15 for high-density disks. You can't use this switch with the /t or /v switches.

Sample

Your department has run out of new high-density (1.2M) 5¼" floppy disks, and you need to copy some files for Al in Finance. You decide to trash an old high-density disk that you find in the Boss's office. To reformat this disk, you enter

```
format a:
```

Later on that day, Sue comes over with a new double-density 5¼" disk and asks you to format it for her (she can't do it because Cindy's doing payroll on her machine). Because you know Sue's computer has only a double-sided floppy drive, you enter the following command to format her disk on your high-density floppy drive:

```
format a: /4
```

Note that you could also accomplish this task by entering

```
format a: /f:360
```

 See the examples in *DOS For Dummies,* Chapter 12, sections "Formatting a Disk," "Formatting a Low-Capacity Disk in a High-Capacity Drive," and "Reformatting Disks."

More stuff

 If you're using DOS Version 5 or later and (knock on wood) you reformat a floppy disk that has valuable data on it, you may be able to recover the files (or most of them anyway) with the UNFORMAT command, provided that you use this command before you put any new files on this disk.

GRAFTABL

 Enables your computer to display special graphics characters on-screen when you have a color/graphics adapter and the computer is in graphics mode.

DOSspeak

GRAFTABL [*xxx* | /status]

Variable or Option	Function
xxx	Specifies the number of the code page whose character set is to be used. Code page numbers include 437 for American (English), 850 for Multilingual, 860 for Portuguese, 863 for French-Canadian, and 865 for Nordic.
/status	Displays the number of the active code page (this can be abbreviated to /sta).

If you enter GRAFTABL without any parameters, DOS lists the number of the previous code page.

Sample

Cousin Olaf wants to use your computer again, this time to compose an old Norse hymn to Odin with lots of strange looking runic characters in it. You obviously need to switch him over to the Nordic code page, so you enter

```
graftabl 865
```

After entering this command, you check to see if your computer is ready for rune(s) by entering

```
graftabl /sta
```

GRAPHICS

Enables you to print a screen containing graphics characters on an IBM-compatible printer with the Print Screen key (a.k.a., Shift-PrtSc).

DOSspeak

GRAPHICS [*type*] [[*drive:*[*path*][*filename*] [/r] [/b] [/lcd] [/printbox:*id*]

Variable or Option	Function
type	Specifies the type of printer (see following table).

[*drive:*[*path*]*filename*	(Versions 4+) Specifies the name of the drive, path, and the printer profile file. If you omit this parameter, DOS uses the GRAPHICS.PRO file.
/r	Reverses the foreground and background in the printout so that it resembles the screen more closely (with white characters on a black background).
/b	Prints the background in color when the *type* parameter is color4 or color8 (see table below).
/lcd	Prints the image from the Liquid Crystal Display (LCD) of an IBM PC Convertible.
/printbox:*id*	(Versions 4+) Specifies the size of the printbox. *id* is the first parameter following the Printbox Statement in your printer profile. When using the GRAPHICS.PRO file for your printer information, the *id* parameter is either std or lcd.

The *type* parameter can be any of the following:

Type	*Printer*
color1	IBM PC Color Printer with a black ribbon or the black band of a color ribbon
color4	IBM PC Color Printer with a red-green-blue-black color ribbon
color8	IBM PC Color Printer with a cyan-magenta-yellow-black color ribbon
compact	(Version 3.3 only) IBM PC Compact Printer
graphics	IBM Personal Graphics Printer, Proprinter, or Quietwriter
graphicswide	(Versions 4+) IBM Personal Graphics Printer, Proprinter, or Quietwriter with wide carriage
thermal	IBM PC Convertible Thermal Printer
hpdefault	(Versions 5+) Any Hewlett-Packard PCL printer
deskjet	(Versions 5+) HP Deskjet
laserjet	(Versions 5+) HP Laserjet
laserjetii	(Versions 5+) HP Laserjet Series II

paintjet	(Versions 5+) HP Paintjet
quietjet	(Versions 5+) HP Quietjet
quietjetplus	(Versions 5+) HP Quietjet Plus
ruggedwriter	(Versions 5+) HP Rugged Writer
ruggedwriterwide	(Versions 5+) HP Rugged Writer with wide carriage
thinkjet	(Versions 5+) HP Thinkjet

If you use GRAPHICS without any parameters, DOS will load the command, using the graphics type parameter (as described in the preceding table).

Sample

You need to print a screen that contains lines and boxes to include in a report. Your printer is an HP Laserjet Series II. Prior to pressing the Print Screen key, you enter

```
graphics laserjetii
```

See the examples in *DOS For Dummies,* Chapter 10, sections "Printing the Screen" and "Print Screen woes."

HELP

In Version 6, starts a menu-driven utility that gives you help information on any DOS command. In earlier versions, displays an alphabetical list of all DOS and batch commands or a short description of a particular command (including the DOSspeak line and a listing of the parameters).

DOSspeak

HELP [*command*]

where *command* is the name of the DOS command you want help information on. To get help on a command right before you execute it (which might be a little risky), type the command followed by the/? switch.

Sample

Suppose that Sue has borrowed your copy of the *DOS For Dummies Quick Reference.* You can't look up the DOSspeak for the FORMAT command, and you've forgotten the switch for formatting a double-sided disk in your high-density drive. To get help on this command, you enter

```
help format
```

After DOS spits up the FORMAT DOSspeak on-screen, you decide
that you really need a printout of this stuff. To send the gobbledygook on FORMAT to your printer rather than your screen, this
time you enter

```
help format >prn
```

INTERLNK

Connects two computers via their parallel or serial ports so that
they can share information and resources like a printer (available
only in DOS 6+).

DOSspeak

INTERLNK [*client*[:]=[*server*][:]]

Variable or Option	Function
client	Specifies the letter of the client drive that is to be redirected to a drive on the Interlnk server. The drive letter you give for the *client* parameter must be one that was redirected when you started Interlnk (see INTERSVR).
server	Specifies the letter of the drive on the Interlnk server that will be redirected. This drive must be one of those listed on the This Computer (Server) column of the Interlnk server screen. If you omit the *server* parameter, Interlnk no longer redirects the client drive specified by the *client* parameter.

If you enter INTERLNK without any parameters, DOS displays the
current status of the interlinked drives.

Sample

Suppose that the Interlnk server is running and drive D is one of
the server drives. To redirect client drive F to drive D on the
server, you enter

```
interlnk f=d
```

Later, to cancel the redirection of client drive F, you enter

```
interlnk f=
```

More stuff

In order to use the INTERLNK command, the INTERLNK.EXE device driver must be installed (see DEVICE in the Configuration Commands section) and the Interlnk server must be running (see INTERSVR).

INTERSVR

Starts the Interlnk server and specifies how the server's drives are to be redirected and which ports are used to connect to the client (available only in DOS 6+).

DOSspeak

To start the Interlnk server:

INTERSVR [*drive:*[...]] [/x=*drive:*[...]]
[/lpt:[*n* | *address*]] [/com:[*n* |*address*]]
[/baud:*rate*] [/b] [/v]

To copy the Interlnk files from one computer to another:

INTERSVR [/rcopy]

Variable or Option	Function
drive:	Specifies the letter(s) of the server drive(s) to be redirected to client drives. If you omit the *drive:* parameter, all server drives are redirected. To specify multiple server drives, separate each drive letter with a space.
/x=*drive*	Specifies the letter(s) of the server drive(s) not to be redirected to a client drive(s). Keep in mind that, by default, all drives are redirected.
/lpt:[*n* | *address*]	Specifies a parallel port to use. You can specify which port to use either with an *n* parameter that specifies the number of the LPT port or an *address* parameter that specifies the port's address. If you omit the *n* or *address* parameter, Interlnk uses the first parallel port that it finds.

/com: [*n* | *address*]	Specifies a serial port to use. You can specify which port to use with either an *n* parameter that specifies the number of the COM port or an *address* parameter that specifies the port's address. If you omit the *n* or *address* parameter, Interlnk uses the first serial port that it finds.
/baud:*rate*	Specifies the baud rate. The *rate* parameter can be any of the following: 9600, 19200, 38400, 57600, or 115200 (the default).
/b	Displays the Interlnk server screen in black and white.
/v	Prevents conflicts with a computer's timer when using a serial connection between computers; one stops running when you use Interlnk to access a drive or printer port.
/rcopy	Copies the Interlnk files from one computer to another when they are connected with a 7-wire, null-modem serial cable (what else would you use?) and the MODE command is available on the computer where you're installing Interlnk.

If you enter INTERSVR without any parameters, DOS starts the Interlnk server and displays the Interlnk server screen using the default display.

Sample

To start the Interlnk server and specify that drives C and A on the server be redirected to the client as drives D and E, respectively, you enter

```
intersvr c: a:
```

More stuff

Before you can use the INTERSVR command, the INTERLNK.EXE device driver must be installed (see DEVICE in the Configuration Commands section). Also, you can't use the INTERSVR command to redirect network drives or drives like CD-ROM drives that use a redirection interface, nor can you use INTERSVR with the CHKDSK, DEFRAG, DISKCOMP, DISKCOPY, FDISK, FORMAT, MIRROR, SYS, UNDELETE, or UNFORMAT commands.

JOIN

Joins a disk drive to a directory on another drive so that the entire directory structure of the disk drive *appears* as a subdirectory on the other drive and *the first drive letter is no longer available.*

DOSspeak

JOIN [*drive1:* [*drive2:*]*path*]

or

JOIN *drive1:* /d

Variable or Option	Function
drive1:	Specifies the drive whose entire directory will appear as a directory on *drive2*.
drive2:	Specifies the drive to which *drive1* is to be joined.
path	Specifies the directory on *drive2* where the *drive1* will appear. This directory must be empty and must not be the *drive2* root directory.
/d	Cancels the join between drive (as does resetting the computer).

If you enter JOIN without any parameters, DOS lists the joins in effect (if none are in effect, nothing is just what DOS displays).

Sample

Suppose that you want to join the disk in drive A to a new (empty) subdirectory called \ALIAS_A that you've created on drive C. To do this crazy thing, you enter

```
join a: c:\alias_a
```

OK, you've had your fun doing directory listings of C:\ALIAS_A and getting a list of the files on drive A. Now, you're ready to sever the connection before you get into some real trouble. To do so, you enter

```
join a: /d
```

More stuff

Stay away from this command unless you're absolutely sure that you know what it is you're doing. Also, even if you do know what you're doing, avoid using this command on any drive under the influence of the ASSIGN or SUBST command.

KEYB

Changes the keyboard layout from the U.S. default to one for a particular foreign language.

DOSspeak

KEYB [*xx*[,[*yyy*][,[*drive:*][*path*]*filename*]]] [/e] [/id:*nnn*]

Variable or Option	Function
xx	Specifies a two-letter keyboard code (see following tables).
yyy	Specifies the code page for the character set (see the second table below).
[*drive:*][*path*]*filename*	Specifies the drive, directory, and name of the file with the keyboard definition file KEYBOARD.SYS. If you omit this parameter, DOS looks for this file in the directories in the search path (see PATH).
/e	(Versions 5+) Specifies that an enhanced keyboard is installed (one of those babies with 101 or 102 keys that you're dying to get your hands on).
/id:*nnn*	(Versions 4+) Specifies the keyboard ID (see second table below) for countries with more than one enhanced keyboard (such as France, Italy, and the UK).

In DOS versions prior to 3.3, the KEYBOARD command uses only the two-letter keyboard codes as shown in the following table. When using one of these codes as the *xx* parameter, the parameter must follow the keyboard command with no spaces — for example, `keybit` to switch to the Italian keyboard layout.

Two-Letter Keyboard Code	Country
uk	United Kingdom
gr	Germany
fr	France
it	Italy
sp	Spain

In DOS Versions 3.3+, you specify both the keyboard code as the *xx* parameter and a code page number as the *yyy* parameter. (Note, however, that the code page numbers are different in Versions 3.3 and 4+.) In Versions 4+, you can also specify a keyboard ID as the *nnn* parameter when a country supports more than one enhanced keyboard. The following table shows all these codes:

Keyboard Code	Code Page Number V3.3 | V4+	Keyboard ID	Keyboard Layout
us	001 | 437	103	USA (the default)
cf	002 | 863	058	Canada (French)
fr	033 | 437	189 or 120	France
gr	049 | 437	129	Germany
it	039 | 437	141 or 142	Italy
sp	034 | 437	172	Spain
uk	044 | 437	166 or 168	United Kingdom
po	351 | 860	163	Portugal
sg	041 | 437	000	Switzerland (German)
sf	041 | 437	150	Switzerland (French)
dk	045 | 865	159	Denmark
be	032 | 437	120	Belgium
nl	031 | 437	143	Netherlands
no	047 | 865	155	Norway
la	003 | 437	171	Latin America
sv	046 | 437	153	Sweden
sv	046 | 437	153	Finland

When you enter KEYB without any parameters, DOS displays the current keyboard code page.

Sample

Cousin Olaf is using your computer again, this time to compose a Norse heroic saga. But he's complaining about what he calls "this fancy pants U S of A keyboard," and he wants the keyboard to act "like the one we use in old country." To switch him over to the Nordic keyboard layout and make him happy, you enter

```
keyb no,865
```

More stuff

In DOS versions prior to 3.3, you can load a new keyboard layout with the KEYB command only once per work session. In later versions, you can use the command as often as necessary to switch to different layouts. In all versions, you can switch back to the default (U.S.) keyboard at any time by pressing Ctrl-Alt-F1; then return to the keyboard layout you loaded with KEYB by pressing Ctrl-Alt-F2.

LABEL

Enables you to add, modify, or delete a volume label from a formatted floppy or hard disk.

DOSspeak

LABEL [*drive* :][*label*]

Variable or Option	Function
drive:	Specifies the letter of the drive containing the disk whose volume label you want to adjust. If you don't specify a *drive:* parameter, DOS assumes that you want to work with the disk in the current drive.
label	Specifies the volume label (up to 11 characters) that you want assigned to the disk specified by the *drive:* parameter. If you don't specify a *label* parameter, DOS displays the current label and prompts you to enter a new one. To delete the label, just press Enter and then press Y to the `Delete current volume label (Y/N)?` prompt.

Sample

Suppose that you didn't assign a label to your floppy disk when you formatted it, but now that you've backed up a number of important spreadsheet files, you want to label the disk SERIOUS_123. To do so, put the floppy disk in drive A and then enter

```
label a: serious_123
```

See the example in *DOS For Dummies,* Chapter 12, section "Changing the Volume Label."

More stuff

You can't use the LABEL command with a drive under the influence of our old friends ASSIGN, JOIN, or SUBST.

LH or LOADHIGH

Loads a terminate-and-stay resident (TSR) program into upper (reserved) memory area on an Intel 386 or 486-based computer. (available in Versions 5+ only).

DOSspeak

LH [*drive:*][*path*]***filename*** [*parameters*]

or

LH [*/l:region1*[*,minsize1*][*;region2*[*,minsize2*]
[*/s*]]=[*drive:*][*path*]***filename*** [*dd-parameters*]

Variable or Option	Function
[*drive:*][*path*]*filename*	Specifies the drive, path, and name of the TSR program command file that you want to load into reserved memory.
parameters	Specifies any command line parameters that the program requires to load.
/l:*region1*[,*minsize1*] [;*region2*[,*minsize2*]	Specifies one or more regions of memory in which the device driver is to be loaded. To ensure that a driver won't be loaded into a region that's too small for it, you can also specify the *minsize* parameter for the particular *region* parameter that you specify.

/s

Normally used by the MemMaker program to shrink the UMB (upper memory block) to its minimum size while the device drive is loading. Don't use this /s switch unless you're certain that shrinking the UMB won't interfere with loading the device driver. You can only use the /s switch with the /l switch and when you've specified both a *region* and *minsize* parameter.

Before you can use the LH (LOADHIGH) command, your CONFIG.SYS (System Configuration) file must first have loaded the HIMEM.SYS device driver plus an expanded memory manager like the EMM386.EXE device driver. See DEVICE in the Configuration Commands section of this reference for more information.

Sample

Today, you're using the 486 computer that your Boss (who's away on business in Europe) uses. You decide that you want to load the DOSKEY utility to make it easier to recall and edit your DOS commands as you work. To load the DOSKEY utility in the reserved memory of the Boss's 486, you enter

```
lh doskey
```

See the example in *DOS For Dummies,* Chapter 7, section "Upper Memory."

More stuff

You don't have to abbreviate this command to LH — if you're really into typing, you can enter LOADHIGH instead.

LOADFIX

Loads a program above the first 64K of conventional memory (Versions 5+ only). Use the LOADFIX command only after you've received a `Packed file corrupt` error message when trying to run an older program under DOS 5+.

DOSspeak

LOADFIX [*drive:*][*path*]***filename***

where [*drive:*][*path*]*filename* specifies the drive, path, and name of the program file that runs the program you want to load with LOADFIX.

More stuff

Most application programs have no need for LOADFIX unless they are truly ancient (in which case, maybe you should upgrade them).

MD or MKDIR

Creates a new directory on your disk.

DOSspeak

MD [*drive:*][*path*]***name***

Variable or Option	Function
drive:	Specifies the drive on whose disk the new directory is to be created.
path	Specifies the existing directory in which the new directory will be created (thus, making the new directory one of the subdirectories of the existing directory).
name	Specifies the name of the new directory. This directory *name* can be no more than eight characters long with a three-character extension (and no spaces) — just like a filename. If you specify a *path* parameter, you must precede the *name* parameter with a \ (backslash). If the name already exists in the location specified by the *drive:* and *path* parameters, DOS gives you the error message Unable to create directory.

Sample

Suppose that you need to create a subdirectory of your \MYTURF directory to store all the legal documents you work with (so you'll call it LEGSTUFF). To create this new directory when your \MYTURF directory is current, you enter

```
md legstuff
```

Now you remember that you also need to create a new directory for your assistant to keep files separate from yours. You want this directory to be on the same level as your \MYTURF directory (right below the root on drive C), and you decide to call it ASTJUNK. To create this directory, you enter

```
md \astjunk
```

See the example in *DOS For Dummies,* Chapter 17, section "How to Name a Directory (the MKDIR Command)."

More stuff

You don't have to abbreviate this command to MD — DOS knows it as MKDIR as well.

MEM

Displays the amount of free and used memory in your computer (available in Versions 4+).

DOSspeak

In versions prior to DOS 6:

> **MEM** [/program | /debug | /classify]

In Version 6:

> **MEM** [/classify | debug | /free |
> /module *programname*] [/page]

Variable or Option	Function
/program	Displays the status of the programs currently loaded into memory. In Versions 5+, you can abbreviate this switch to /p.
/debug	Displays the status of the programs and system device drivers currently loaded into memory. In Versions 5+, you can abbreviate this switch to /d.
/classify	(Versions 5+) Classifies programs by their memory usage. Displays the size of the programs and gives you a summary of memory usage. You can abbreviate this switch to /c.
/free	Lists the free areas of conventional and upper memory. You can use this switch with /page but not with the other switches; you can abbreviate it to /f.

| /module *programname* | Shows how a program name is currently using memory; you must specify the *programname* parameter with the /module switch. You can use this switch with /page but not with the other switches; you can abbreviate it to /m. |
| /page | Pauses after each screenful of information. |

Sample

Suppose that you're working at the Boss's 486 machine and you suddenly become curious about just how much raw RAM this baby packs. To display the amount of used and free memory with the program classified by memory usage, you enter

```
mem /c
```

See the example in *DOS For Dummies,* Chapter 7, section "Conventional Memory."

More stuff

If you're using a version of DOS prior to 4.0, you can use the CHKDSK command to see how much memory your computer has.

MEMMAKER

Starts the MemMaker program, which optimizes a 386 or 486 computer's memory by moving device drivers and terminate-and-stay-resident (TSR) programs to upper memory (available only in DOS 6+).

DOSspeak

MEMMAKER [/b] [/batch] [/session] [/swap:*drive*] [/t] [/undo] [/w:*size1*,*size2*]

Variable or Option	Function
/b	Displays MemMaker in black and white. Use this switch when the program isn't displayed correctly on a monochrome monitor.

/batch	Runs MemMaker in batch (unattended) mode where the program supplies the default responses to each prompt. If an error occurs, MemMaker restores your previous AUTOEXEC.BAT and CONFIG.SYS files and, if necessary, Windows SYSTEM.INI files. After the batch process is complete, you can review the session in a file called MEMMAKER.STS that you can open with the DOS Editor (see EDIT).
/session	This switch is used only by MemMaker when optimizing your computer's memory.
/swap:*drive*	Specifies that the drive letter for the startup disk has changed since booting your computer (some disk compression utilities change startup drive letters when they swap compressed and uncompressed files). Specify the modified drive letter as the /swap *drive* parameter. Don't use this switch with the Stacker 2.0, SuperStor, or Microsoft DoubleSpace — see DBLSPACE (Compress) — compression utilities.
/t	Disables the detection of IBM Token-Ring networks so that you can use MemMaker on such a network.
/undo	Undoes the most recent changes to your AUTOEXEC.BAT, CONFIG.SYS and, if affected, Windows SYSTEM.INI files. Then you can return to your previous memory configuration if you're not satisfied with the job MemMaker did.
/w:*size1,size2*	Specifies how much upper memory space to reserve for Windows translation buffers. The *size1* parameter specifies how much memory to reserve for the first translation buffer area; the *size2* parameter specifies how much to reserve for the second area (the default is no upper memory for the Windows translation buffers).

If you enter MEMMAKER without any parameters, DOS starts the MemMaker program, which prompts you for the drivers and memory-resident programs to load into upper memory.

Sample

To run the MemMaker program on your Boss's 486 computer in
batch mode, you enter

```
memmaker /batch
```

Later, your Boss indicates a preference for the computer before
you optimized the memory. To restore the previous memory
configuration, you enter

```
memmaker /undo
```

More stuff

Don't use the MEMMAKER command while you are running
Microsoft Windows.

MIRROR

 Records disk information about a specified drive that the
UNFORMAT command can later use to help recover its files —
that's if you just happen to reformat the disk (oops!) by mistake
(available in Version 5 only).

DOSspeak

```
MIRROR [drive:[ ...]] [/1] [/tdrive[-entries][ ...]]
```

or

```
MIRROR [/u]
```

or

```
MIRROR [/partn]
```

Variable or Option	Function
drive:	Specifies the drive whose file and directory information you want to save. To specify more than one drive, separate each *drive:* parameter by a space. If you omit the *drive:* parameter, DOS uses the current drive.
/1	Saves only the latest disk information in the MIRROR.FIL file in the root directory specified by the *drive:* parameter (does not save a backup called MIRROR.BAK).

/tdrive	Loads the deletion-tracking program for the *drive* specified after the /t switch. This program saves information each time you delete a file in the specified *drive* in a special file called PCTRACKR.DEL, which is located in the root directory of the *drive*.
-entries	Specifies the number of entries the deletion-tracking program will save. Default values for the *-entries* parameter vary according to the size of the disk specified by the *drive* parameter (see the following table).
/u	Unloads the deletion-tracking program.
/partn	Saves hard disk partition information in a file named PARTNSAV.FIL on a floppy disk.

As you can see from the following table, not only does the default number of entries saved by the deletion-tracking program vary according to the type of disk specified by the t/*drive* parameter but so does the resulting size of the PCTRACKR.DEL file (yeoww!).

Type of Disk	Default Number of Entries	Size of the PCTRACKR.DEL File
360K	25	5K
720K	50	9K
1.2M	75	14K
1.44M	75	15K
20M	101	18K
32M	202	36K
over 32M	303	55K

Sample

To record disk information about your hard disk (drive C) and load the deletion-tracking program, you enter

```
mirror /tc
```

More stuff

Even if you don't use the MIRROR command to record information about your disk, it may still be possible to recover your files (at least some of them) with the UNFORMAT command — see UNFORMAT later in this DOS Commands section for more information.

Don't use the MIRROR command on a drive under the influence of the JOIN or SUBST command.

MODE (Codepage)

Prepares and selects a code page (that is, a foreign character set) for a particular device.

DOSspeak

To prepare the code page for use with a particular device:

MODE *device* codepage prepare=((*yyy*[...]) [*drive:*][*path*]*filename*)

To select the code page and make it active for a particular device:

MODE *device* codepage select=*yyy*

To restore a previously selected code page to a particular device:

MODE *device* codepage refresh

To display information on the current code page status for a particular device:

MODE *device* codepage [/status]

Variable or Option	Function
device	Specifies the device which uses the code page. The *device* parameter can be CON (your console [monitor]), PRN (printer), LPT1 (printer on 1st parallel port) , LPT2 (printer on 2nd parallel port), or LPT3 (printer on 3rd parallel port).
yyy	Specifies the number of the code page to be used with the device. The *yyy* parameter can be 437 for American (English), 850 for Multilingual, 860 for Portuguese, 863 for French-Canadian, or 865 for Nordic.
[*drive:*][*path*]*filename*	Specifies the drive, path, and name of the file with the code page information. When you omit the *drive:* and *path* parameters, DOS assumes that the file is located in the directories included in your path (see PATH).

In Version 3.3, the *filename* parameter can be EGA.CPI (for an EGA or VGA graphics adapter), LCD.CPI (for the IBM PC Convertible Liquid Crystal Display), 4201.CPI (for the IBM 4201 Proprinter family), 4208.CPI (for the IBM Proprinter X24 and XL24), or 5202.CPI (for the IBM Quietwriter III). Later versions of DOS can include other files (check your documentation for specifics). When entering the *filename* parameter, you can omit the CPI extension because it is assumed.

/status

(Versions 4+) This parameter is completely superfluous. If you feel that you just have to use it, you can abbreviate it to /sta rather than type the whole /status thing out.

Sample

Cousin Olaf wants to print his old Norse hymn to Odin on your printer. To get all the strange runic characters, you need to prepare code page 850 for your printer:

```
mode prn codepage prepare=(850) c:\dos\5202.cpi
```

After preparing the code page, you select it for your printer as follows:

```
mode prn codepage select=850
```

To make sure that your printer is now set up for Cousin Olaf, you then enter

```
mode prn codepage
```

More stuff

When using the MODE command to prepare, select, or refresh a code page or get status information on the code page for a device, you can abbreviate the codepage parameter to cp. Also, when preparing a code page, you can abbreviate the prepare parameter to prep.

MODE (Configure Printer)

Specifies the number of columns and lines for a printer connected to one of your parallel ports.

DOSspeak

MODE LPT*n*[:][*c*][,[*l*][,p]]

or (in Versions 4+)

MODE LPT*n*[:] [cols=*c*] [lines=*l*] [retry=*r*]

Variable or Option	Function
LPT*n*	Specifies the number of the parallel port (1, 2, or 3) to which your printer is attached. (LPT stands for line printer.)
c	Specifies the number of columns (and characters) to print per line. The *c* parameter can be 80 or 132 (with 80 as the default).
l	Specifies the number of lines to print per inch. The *l* parameter can be 6 or 8 (with 6 as the default).
p	(Version 3.3 and earlier) Causes DOS to continuously retry to send the output when the printer is not ready (equivalent to retry=b in later versions — see next option).
r	(Versions 4+) Specifies the retry action that DOS should take when the printer is busy. The *r* parameter can be e (for return error), b (for return busy), r (for return ready), or none (to take no action).

Sample

Today, you're working at Cindy's computer and she has a wide-carriage printer. You just tried printing a file from DOS, and you notice that the printout uses only the first 80 columns. Before you reprint the file, set the mode for Cindy's printer to 132 columns to take full advantage of the wide carriage and tell DOS to resend the print info if the printer is not ready (like when you forget to put the printer back on line) by entering

```
mode lpt1 cols=132 retry=b
```

Unfortunately, when you press Enter, DOS gives you a nasty error message because Cindy's machine still uses Version 3.3 (when is she going to get with it?). To get her older version of DOS to listen to you, you rephrase the MODE command to

```
mode lpt1:132,,p
```

The extra comma indicates where you would put the number of
lines per inch if you were changing this parameter — it must be
there in Version 3.3 when you want to use the p (retry busy)
parameter.

MODE (Configure Serial Port)

Specifies the parameters for a serial (communications) port that
define the speed and how the data are transmitted.

DOSspeak

MODE COM*m*[:]*b*[[,*p*[,*d*][,*s*[,*p*]]]]

or (in Versions 4+)

MODE COM*m*[:] [baud=*b*] [parity=*p*] [data=*d*]
[stop=*s*] [retry=*r*]

Variable or Option	Function
COM*m*	Specifies the number of the serial (communications) port (1, 2, 3, or 4) to which the device is attached (the COM in COM1, COM2, and so on, stands for communications because these ports are often used to connect to devices, such as a modem, to your computer).
b	Specifies the baud rate (that is, the bits per second). The *b* parameter can be 110, 150, 300, 600, 1200, 2400, 4800, 9600, or 19200. You must specify a baud rate because there is no default.
p	Specifies the parity (error checking). The *p* parameter can be n (for none), o (for odd), or e (for even); also m (for mark) or s (for space) in Versions 4+. The default is e (for even).
d	Specifies the number of data bits. The *d* parameter can be 7 or 8; also 5 or 6 in Versions 4+. The default is 7 data bits.
s	Specifies the number of stop bits. The *s* parameter can be 1 or 2; also 1.5 in Versions 4+. If the *b* parameter is 110, *s* is 2 by default. Otherwise, the default is 1.

p   (Versions 3.3 and earlier) Causes DOS to continuously retry sending the output when the serial port is not ready (equivalent to `retry=b` in later versions — see the following).

r   (Versions 4+) Specifies the retry action that DOS should take when the serial port is busy. The *r* parameter can be e (for return error — the default), b (for return busy), r (for return ready), or none (to take no action).

Sample

When Mr. Peters retired, Sue inherited his old Diablo serial printer. She wants you (of all people) to help her configure DOS so that she can print with the fossil printer. You finally decipher from her printer manual that baud rate should be set to 2400, the parity to None, data bits to 8, and stop bits to 1. To set up her first serial port for this printer, you enter

```
mode com1 baud=2400 parity=n data=8 stop=1
```

Unfortunately, when you press Enter, DOS gives you a nasty error message because Sue's still using Version 3.3 on her old klunker. To get this version of DOS to listen to you, you have to reenter the MODE command as

```
mode com1:2400,n,8,1
```

See the example in *DOS For Dummies,* Chapter 10, section "The Serial Connection."

More stuff

If you're specifying a printer for your COM port, in addition to setting up the port settings with the MODE command, you also need to redirect the printer — see MODE (Redirect Parallel Printer) for details.

MODE (Device Status)

Displays current status information on a particular device on your system (Versions 4+).

DOSspeak

MODE [*device*] [/status]

Variable or Option	Function
device	Specifies the device for which you want the status information. The *device* parameter can be CON (your console [monitor]), PRN (printer), LPT1 (printer on 1st parallel port), LPT2 (printer on 2nd parallel port), LPT3 (printer on 3rd parallel port), COM1 (1st serial port), COM2 (2nd serial port), COM3 (3rd serial port), or COM4 (4th serial port).
/status	This parameter is not required unless you are requesting the status of a redirected parallel printer — see MODE (Redirect Parallel Printer). You can abbreviate this parameter to /sta.
	If you enter MODE without any parameters, DOS gives you information on all the devices that are installed in your system.

Sample

To check the status of your first parallel port, you enter

```
mode lpt1
```

To check the status of this parallel port after you redirected it to your first serial port, you enter

```
mode lpt1 /sta
```

MODE (Display)

Selects the display and controls how the information is displayed.

DOSspeak

To select the display:

MODE [*display-adapter*][*,n*]

or

MODE CON[:] [cols=*c*] [lines=*n*]

To select a display and shift the image with CGA graphics:

MODE [*display-adapter*][*,shift*[*,t*]]

Variable or Option	Function
CON[:]	Indicates the display monitor.
display-adapter	Specifies the type of display. The *display-adapter* parameter can be mono (for monochrome adapter, 80 columns), 40 (for color/graphics adapter, 40 columns), 80 (for color/graphics adapter, 80 columns), bw40 (for color/graphics adapter, 40 columns with color disabled), bw80 (for color/graphics adapter, 80 columns with color disabled), co40 (for color/graphics adapter, 40 columns with color enabled), and co80 (for color/ graphics adapter, 80 columns with color enabled).
n	(Versions 4+) Specifies the number of lines on the display. The *n* parameter varies according to the adapter and its settings. Typical values include 25, 43, and 50 (check your monitor documentation for permissible values).
c	(Versions 4+) Specifies the number of columns (that is, characters) that appear on each line on the display. The *c* parameter can be 40 or 80.
shift	Specifies whether to shift the screen display to the left (l) or right (r) when adjusting a display connected to a CGA adapter (this command does not work with EGA or VGA color/graphics adapters). When you specify *r* as the shift parameter, DOS shifts the display two columns to the right on an 80-column display or one column to the right on a 40-column display. When you specify *l* as this parameter, DOS adjusts the display the same amount but in the opposite (left) direction.
t	Causes DOS to display a test pattern that you can shift to the left or right until the display is aligned properly on your monitor.

Sample

To display 43-lines on your 16-inch color monitor attached to a EGA graphics card, you enter

```
mode con lines=43
```

See the example in *DOS For Dummies,* Chapter 8, section "Funky Displays."

MODE (Keyboard Typematic Rate)

Controls the rate at which the keys on your keyboard repeat (the so-called typematic effect) and the initial delay before the typematic effect kicks in.

DOSspeak

> **MODE** CON[:] [rate=*r* delay=*d*]

Variable or Option	Function
CON[:]	Indicates the display monitor.
r	Specifies the rate at which a key repeats. The *r* parameter can be between 2 and 32, representing characters per second.
d	Specifies the initial delay before the key repeats. The *d* parameter can be 1 (for ¼ of a second), 2 (for ½ of a second), 3 (for ¾ of a second) or 4 (for a full second).

Sample

To reduce the typematic interval to 15 (20 is the default) and increase the initial delay to ½ second (from the ¼ default), you enter

```
mode con rate=15 delay=2
```

See the example in *DOS For Dummies,* Chapter 9, section "Controlling the Keyboard."

MODE (Redirect Parallel Printer)

Redirects the output from a parallel port to a printer connected to a serial (communications) port after using the MODE command to configure the serial port — see MODE (Configure Serial Port).

DOSspeak

> **MODE LPT***n*[:]=**COM***m*[:]

Variable or Option	Function
LPT*n*[:]	Specifies the number of the parallel port whose output is to be redirected. The *n* parameter can be 1, 2, or 3.
COM*m*[:]	Specifies the number of the serial port to which the output is redirected. The *m* parameter can be 1, 2, 3, or 4.

Sample

After you finish configuring Sue's COM1 serial port for her new, hand-me-down Diablo serial printer, you redirect the printer output to this port by entering

```
mode lpt1=com1
```

MORE

Instructs DOS to display text one screenful at time rather than in one big scrolling blur.

DOSspeak

> **more** < [*drive:*][*path*]***filename***

or

> ***command*** | **MORE**

When using the MORE command to control the display of a text file, you can either redirect input from the disk file, for example

```
more < read.me
```

or "pipe" the output of the TYPE command to the MORE command, for example

```
type read.me | more
```

The vertical bar (the shifted \ key) is called the pipe character, and it sends the result of one DOS command to another.

Sample

You've just gotten a new program. Before you install it, the documentation tells you to read a file called SETUP.TXT. When you use the TYPE command to display this file, pages and pages of stuff fly by in one big blur. To display this file a readable screen at a time, you enter

```
type setup.txt | more
```

You can also do this by entering

```
more < setup.txt
```

This time, DOS stops after displaying each screenful and waits before displaying the next screen until you press a key (any key).

MOVE

Moves one or more files to a new location on a disk. You can also use this DOS command to rename a directory on your disk.

DOSspeak

> **MOVE** [*drive:*][*path*]**filename**
> [,[*drive:*][*path*]filename[...]] ***destination*** [/-y] [/y]

Variable or Option	Function
[*drive:*][*path*]*filename*	Specifies the drive, directory, and names of the file(s) to be moved or the name of the directory to be renamed. Instead of listing the files individually, separated with + signs, you can use wildcard characters in the filenames.
destination	Specifies the new location of the file(s) you're moving or the new name of the directory you're renaming. The *destination* parameter can consist of a drive letter and colon, directory name, or a combination of the two. If you want to rename a file or group of files, you can specify a *filename* parameter as well.
/-y	Forces the MOVE command to prompt you before overwriting an existing file.
/y	Allows the MOVE command to overwrite existing files without prompting.

Sample

Suppose that you want to move a file called BUNK.DOC that's currently in your C:\MYTURF directory to a new directory called C:\NEWSTUFF. To do so, enter

```
move c:\myturf\bunk.doc c:\newstuff
```

More stuff

Be careful! Moving a file to a location that contains a file with the same name will wipe out the existing file in that location.

MSAV

Scans your computer for known viruses and then removes the viruses detected and/or reports back on them (available only in DOS 6+).

DOSspeak

MSAV [*drive:*] [/s] [/c] [/r] [/a] [/l] [/n] [/p] [/f] [/*video*]

Variable or Option	Function
drive:	Specifies the disk that you want MSAV to scan for viruses.
/s	Scans the disk specified by the *drive:* parameter but does not remove the viruses that MSAV finds.
/c	Scans the disk specified by the *drive:* parameter and removes the viruses that MSAV finds.
/r	Creates an MSAV.RPT file that lists the number of files MSAV checked, the number of viruses found, and the number of viruses removed. This report is placed in the root directory of the disk specified by the *drive:* parameter.
/a	Scans all drives except A or B.
/l	Scans all local drives except network drives.
/n	Displays the contents of the MSAV.TXT file, if this file is located in the same directory as the one that contains the MSAV.EXE file; then scans the disk specified by the drive parameter. If MSAV finds a virus, it returns exit code 86 instead of displaying a message on your screen.
/p	Displays a command line instead of the normal GUI (graphical user interface) display.
/f	Turns off the display of names of the files that have been scanned. Use this switch only with the /n or /p switches.
/*video*	Sets the way the MSAV program is displayed on-screen.

You can specify any of the following as the */video* parameter:

/video Parameter	Function
25	Sets the screen display to 25 lines (the default).
28	Sets the screen display to 28 lines (use with VGA graphics adapters).
43	Sets the screen display to 43 lines (use with EGA and VGA graphics adapters).
50	Sets the screen display to 50 lines (use with VGA graphics adapters only).
60	Sets the screen display to 60 lines (use with Video 7 graphics adapters only).
in	Runs MSAV in a color scheme even when a color display adapter is not detected.
bw	Runs MSAV in a black-and-white color scheme.
mono	Runs MSAV in a monochrome color scheme even when a color display adapter is detected.
lcd	Runs MSAV using shades of gray designed for a Liquid Crystal Display (LCD) screen.
ff	Specifies the fastest screen updating on computers using CGA (color/graphics) display adapters.
bf	Uses the computer's BIOS to display video.
nf	Disables the use of alternate fonts with the MSAV program.
bt	Enables the use of a mouse in Windows.
ngm	Runs MSAV displaying the mouse pointer (the arrow pointing left) instead of a graphics character (a rectangle).
le	Switches the left and right mouse buttons.
ps2	Resets the mouse if the mouse pointer disappears or locks up.

If you enter MSAV without any parameters, DOS loads MSAV and scans the current drive for known viruses.

Sample

To start MSAVE in monochrome mode on your color monitor, scan drive C for any known viruses and remove them, and then list the files affected in a report, you enter

```
msav /c /r /mono
```

More stuff

See also VSAFE, a DOS 6 command that continuously scans for viruses.

MSBACKUP

Runs the Microsoft Backup utility, a menu-driven program that enables you to back up your files without typing a single DOS command beyond MSBACKUP (sorry, only DOS 6 offers this utility!).

DOSspeak

MSBACKUP [*setup_file*] [/bw | /lcd | /mda]

Variable or Option	Function
setup_file	Specifies the setup file that defines files to back up and the type of backup.
/bw	Starts the MS Backup program with a black-and-white screen.
/lcd	Starts the MS Backup program in shades of gray for a Liquid Crystal Display (LCD).
/mda	Starts MS Backup in a monochrome display.

The first time you use the MSBACKUP command, you must configure the program for your system. To do this configuration, you will need two or more floppy disks handy. Follow all the screen prompts closely, or better still, get someone who really understands DOS to do this part while you watch.

Sample

It's high time to do a full backup of your hard disk onto floppy disks. Now that you have DOS 6 on your system, you finally decide to bite the bullet. To back up your entire hard disk, you enter

```
msbackup
```

at the DOS prompt. Then follow these steps:

1. Press Alt-B at the first screen to select the Backup button.
2. At the main screen, press Alt-K and select [-C-] as the drive in the Backup From box.

3. Press Alt-Y and select Full as the Backup Type.

4. Press Alt-A and select the floppy drive letter and type of floppy disk to back up to.

5. Finally, put your first blank floppy disk in the backup drive and then press Alt-S to start the backup.

6. Follow the prompts and beeps as you feed disk after disk (you have a big hard drive).

7. After the backup is done, exit the Backup program by choosing the Quit button (press Alt-FX if you're not at the first screen) to return to your old friend the DOS prompt.

More stuff

If you don't yet have Version 6, you can use the good old standby BACKUP command (yuk!) — see BACKUP earlier in this DOS Commands section. Note, however, when you back up files with MSBACKUP, you must use the Microsoft Backup program to restore them as described in *DOS For Dummies*, Chapter 19, section "Restoring using DOS 6's overrated MSBACKUP command."

MSD (Diagnostics)

Starts the Microsoft Diagnostic utility that analyzes your system and tells you all sorts of neat stuff about it, such as how much memory your machine has, what version of DOS you're using, the type of video adapter you have, the number of disk drives you have, and the number of LPT (parallel) and COM (serial) ports you have (available in Versions 5+ only).

DOSspeak

MSD

Sample

You're using the 486 computer again (the Boss is in Outer Mongolia on business — what a job!), and you become curious about just how this PC is configured. To get the lowdown on the system, you enter

```
msd
```

NLSFUNC

National Language Support Function: gets DOS ready for code page switching (that is, using a foreign language character set).

DOSspeak

NLSFUNC [*drive:*][*path*][*filename*]

where [*drive:*][*path*][*filename*] specifies the drive, directory, and name of the file containing the country information (including such things as the time and date formats and currency symbol). If you omit the *drive:* and *path* parameters, DOS searches for this file in your DOS search path (see PATH). If you omit the *filename* parameter, DOS uses the COUNTRY.SYS file.

Sample

Cousin Olaf is in a funk because he can't get access to the Nordic code page with the CHCP 850 command. To remedy this situation, you remember that you first need to get DOS in the mood for code page switching by entering the command

```
nlsfunc
```

which promptly puts DOS in a National Language Support funk!

More stuff

You must use the NLSFUNC command before you use the CHCP (change code page) command to switch to a new code page. However, you only need to use it once per work session. If you have a Cousin Olaf (or some other reason to use code pages), you should put this command in your AUTOEXEC.BAT file.

PATH

Specifies the search path where DOS is to look for all executable (command) files when you issue a DOS command or start an application program.

DOSspeak

PATH [*drive:*][*path*[; . . .]]

or

PATH [;]	
Variable or Option	*Function*
drive:	Specifies the drive on which to set the search path. If you omit the *drive:* parameter, DOS assumes you mean the current drive.
path	Specifies the directories and subdirectories to include in the search path.
;	Separates search paths. When used alone, it cancels the search path previously set with the PATH command.

If you enter PATH without any parameters, DOS displays the current search path.

Sample

You need to set the search path on your computer to include your \DOS and \123 directories so that the computer doesn't burp at you when you enter a particular DOS command or try to start 1-2-3 when you don't happen to be in the \DOS or the \123 directory. To do so, you enter

```
path c:\dos;c:\123
```

More stuff

The PATH command that specifies all the directories and subdirectories you want in your search path is something you should put in your AUTOEXEC.BAT file; then DOS will establish this search path each time you power up your computer.

POWER

Turns on and off the power management utility that sets the levels of power conservation and reports on its status. This command is useful when running laptop computers on battery power (available only in DOS 6+).

DOSspeak

POWER [adv[:max | reg | min]]

or

POWER std | off

Variable or Option	Function
adv[:max | reg | min]	Sets the power conservation setting when the computer's programs and hardware are idle. Specify *max* for maximum power conservation. Specify *reg* to balance power conservation with computer performance (the default). Specify *min* to maximize performance over power conservation.
std	Conserves power by using the power management feature's of your hardware if your computer supports the APM (Advanced Power Management) specification. If your computer doesn't support APM, this parameter turns off power management.
off	Turns off power management.

If you enter POWER without parameters, DOS displays the current power settings.

Sample

To turn on the power management on your laptop computer and maximize power conservation, you enter

```
power adv:max
```

More stuff

You must use the DEVICE command in your CONFIG.SYS file to install the POWER.EXE device drive before you can use the POWER command (see DEVICE in the Configuration Commands section).

PRINT

Prints a text file in the background so that you're free to use more DOS commands (what fun!).

DOSspeak

PRINT [/d:*device*] [/b:*size*] [/u:*ticks*] [/m:*ticks2*]
[/s:*ticks3*] [/q:*qsize*] [/t][*drive:*][*path*]
filename[...] [/c] [/p]

Variable or Option	Function
/d:*device*	Specifies the printer to use (default is PRN). The device parameter can be LPT1 through LPT3 or COM1 through COM4. If you omit the /d switch, DOS prompts you to enter the device name before printing.
/b:*size*	Specifies the size in bytes of the print buffer (default is 512K and the maximum size is 16,384K). The larger the buffer, the more files you can print and the less RAM you have free.
/u:*ticks*	Specifies the amount of time (the number of clock ticks) that the PRINT command waits for a busy printer before giving up its time slice (the default is 1 and the range is between 1 and 255).
/m:*ticks2*	Specifies the maximum amount of time (the number of clock ticks) that the PRINT command keeps control during its time slice (the default is 2 and the range is between 1 and 255).
/s:*ticks3*	Specifies the maximum number of time slices per second during which the PRINT command controls the operating system (the default is 8 and the range is between 1 and 255).
/q:*size*	Specifies the maximum number of files that the print queue can hold (the default is 10 and the range is between 1 and 32).
/t	Stops all printing and empties the print queue (if a file is printing when you give the PRINT command with this switch, DOS stops printing the page and advances the page to the next top of form).

[*drive:*][*path*]*filename*	Specifies the drive, directory, and name of the file(s) to print. To print multiple files, list the filenames separated by spaces or include wildcard characters in the *filename* parameter.
/c	Cancels the printing of the filename that precedes this /c switch, plus all subsequent filenames, until DOS encounters a filename followed by the /p switch.
/p	Adds the filename that precedes this /p switch, plus all subsequent filenames, until DOS encounters a filename followed by the /c switch.

If you enter PRINT without any other parameters, DOS displays a list of files in the print queue.

Sample

You have three files in your \MYTURF directory that you want to print from DOS, TWIDDLE.TXT, TWADDLE.TXT, and TATTLE.TXT. To print them in the background when \MYTURF is the current directory, you enter

```
print twiddle.txt twaddle.txt tattle.txt
```

After giving this command, you realize that you meant to print your TITTLE.TXT file instead of the TATTLE.TXT file. To remove TATTLE.TXT from the queue and print TITTLE.TXT instead, you then enter

```
print tattle.txt /c tittle.txt /p
```

More stuff

Don't use this command on a drive under the influence of the ASSIGN command. Also, don't issue it from a second copy of the DOS command interpreter (started with COMMAND) because it will probably cause your computer to crash and burn rather than your files to print.

PROMPT

Enables you to enhance the (fairly unhelpful) standard DOS prompt (you know, that bland A>, B>, C> thing) to something more exciting (or at least more informative).

DOSspeak

PROMPT [*text*]

where *text* is composed of the following special $ characters or a combination of the text and these characters:

$ character	What you get for your $
$t	The current time as returned by the TIME command.
$d	The current date as returned by the DATE command.
$p ✓	The current drive and directory; for example, C:\MYTURF.
$v	The DOS version as returned by the VER command.
$n	The current drive letter, such as A or C (without the usual colon).
$g	The > character; for example, C> in the normal DOS prompt.
$l	The < character, which would change the normal DOS prompt to C< (ugh).
$b	The	(pipe) character, which would change the normal DOS prompt to C| (still not right).
$q	The = (equal) sign, which would change the normal DOS prompt to C= (a little better).
$h	A backspace, which deletes whatever character precedes it in the *text* parameter.
$e	The Escape character (which appears on-screen like ¨).
$_ (underscore)	Places whatever follows in the *text* parameter on a new line. Use the $_ (make sure that you shift the hyphen) to create a prompt with two or more lines.
$$	Puts the dollar sign ($) in your DOS prompt.

If you enter the PROMPT command without a *text* parameter, DOS sets the prompt back to that bland old A>, B greater than, or C> thing.

Sample

You're tired of the cold and impersonal standard DOS prompt.
You want to see something a little friendlier like

```
What's a gorgeous thing like you doing in a
directory like C:\>?
```

To create this two-line DOS prompt on your computer, you enter

```
prompt What's a gorgeous thing like you
doing!$_in a directory like $p$g?
```

Al in Finance doesn't feel DOS shows him the proper respect, so
he wants to change the DOS prompt to something a tad more
courteous like

```
Master, what is thy bidding in directory C:\>?
```

To create this two-line prompt on his computer, he enters

```
prompt Master, what is thy bidding $_in
directory $p$g?
```

 See the example in *DOS For Dummies,* Chapter 2, section "Prompt
Styles of the Rich and Famous."

More stuff

If you come up with a favorite DOS prompt that you want to see
day in and day out, put the PROMPT command in your
AUTOEXEC.BAT file. Also, when creating a new prompt, add an
extra space after the last character in the *text* parameter to
separate it from the flashing underscore where you start entering
your DOS command.

QBASIC

Starts Microsoft QBasic where you can code basic programs (you
do want to be a programmer, don't you?).

DOSspeak

```
QBASIC [/b] [/editor] [/g] [/h] [/mbf] [/nohi]
[[/run] [drive:][path]filename]
```

Variable or Option	Function
/b	Forces QBasic to be displayed in monochrome on a color monitor (helpful if you're coding on a laptop with an LCD screen).

/editor	Starts the DOS Editor — see EDIT.
/g	Provides fastest possible screen response when running QBasic with a CGA (color/graphics) adapter.
/h	Displays the maximum number of lines possible on your monitor.
/mbf	Causes numbers to be read and stored in Microsoft binary format.
/nohi	Suppresses the display of high intensity video while using QBasic. (Don't use this on laptops because it routinely causes them to have seizures and crash.)
/run	Causes QBasic to run the QBasic file specified by the *filename* parameter before loading it into the Editor.
[*drive:*][*path*]*filename*	Specifies the drive, directory, and the name of an existing QBasic file that you either want to run (with the /run switch) or edit the new basic file you want to code.

If you enter QBASIC without any parameters, DOS starts the QBasic editing screen where you can press Enter to see the Survival Guide (sounds like fun, huh?) or press Esc to start coding a new Basic program.

Sample

Like it or not, you have this bizarre urge to *program in Basic* that you just can't control! Finally, you give in to this perverse craving and start work on a new program file called MYPROG.BAS. To create this file when you start the QBasic program, you enter the command

```
qbasic myprog
```

This command starts the QBasic program and puts you in a new file called MYPROG.BAS (the program automatically appends the BAS extension to the filename) where you can now indulge yourself in this sordid "coding" thing till the cows come home.

RD or RMDIR

Deletes an empty directory from a disk.

DOSspeak

RD [*drive:*]***path***

Variable or Option	Function
drive:	Specifies the drive that contains the disk with the directory you want to get rid of. If you omit this parameter, DOS assumes you mean the current drive.
path	Specifies the name of the directory you want to get rid of. You must specify this parameter, and the directory you specify must be empty of all files and subdirectories before RD can do its stuff.

Sample

You finally decide that it's time to get rid of your NONSENSE directory (as you long ago got rid of the nonsense that was in it). To delete this now empty, unused, and unloved subdirectory of the \MYTURF directory on your hard disk, you enter

```
rd nonsense
```

Unfortunately, when you press Enter, you get this really ambiguous error message `Invalid path, not directory, or directory not empty` (talk about hedging your bets). You look at the DOS prompt and realize the error of your ways: the NONSENSE directory is the current directory. Because DOS can't remove a directory while you're in it, you type `cd..` to go up a level to the \MYTURF directory. Now, when you repeat your RD command, it works like a charm.

More stuff

DOS will also accept RMDIR instead of RD, if you're really into typing. No matter how you enter this command, be very careful with it because there is no way to undelete a deleted directory. If you do take out a directory in error, you have to restore it from backup disks (see BACKUP and RESTORE) or re-create it (see MD or MKDIR).

RECOVER

Recovers files that have bad sectors or reconstructs files from a disk that has a damaged directory structure (versions prior to Version 6 only).

DOSspeak

> **RECOVER** [*drive:*][*path*]***filename***

or

> **RECOVER** *drive:*

Variable or Option	*Function*
[*drive:*][*path*]*filename*	Specifies the drive, directory, and name of the file to recover.
drive:	Specifies the disk that you want reconstructed.

Beware! In the earliest versions of DOS, if you enter RECOVER without any parameters, DOS assumes that you want to recover all the files on the current drive (which often is your hard disk, drive C, and could result in a really big, bad mess).

More stuff

Don't be misled — although RECOVER sounds innocuous enough, it can wreak havoc on your disk if applied to files that aren't already trashed. Therefore, don't play around with the RECOVER command and don't confuse it with the RESTORE command that you use when you need to copy files onto the disk from which they were backed up. Also, don't use RECOVER on a disk under the influence of the JOIN or SUBST command and don't try to use it on a network drive.

✓ *REN or RENAME*

Renames a file or group of files.

DOSspeak

> **REN** [*drive:*][*path*]***filename1 filename2***

Variable or Option	*Function*
[*drive:*][*path*]*filename1*	Specifies the drive, directory, and name of the file you want to rename. If you omit the *drive:* and *path* parameters, DOS assumes the file's in the current drive. To rename multiple files, use wildcard characters in the *filename1* parameter.

filename2	Specifies the new name for the file. When renaming multiple files, use wildcard characters in the *filename2* parameter. You cannot, however, include a *drive:* and *path* parameter with *filename2* — the renamed file must remain in the same location. (Use COPY when you want both to rename and relocate a file.)

Sample

You have a file named HILUCRE.WK1 in your \123STUFF directory that you want to rename BIGBUCKS.WK1. To rename it while you're in your \MYTURF directory, you enter

```
ren c:\123stuff\hilucre.wk1 bigbucks.wk1
```

 See the example in *DOS For Dummies,* Chapter 3, section "Renaming a File."

More stuff

DOS will accept RENAME as the command name if you prefer it over the REN abbreviation.

REPLACE

Selectively adds or replaces files from one disk or directory to another.

DOSspeak

REPLACE [*drive1:*][*path1*]*filename* [*drive2:*][*path2*] [/a] [/p] [/r] [/s] [/w] [/u]

Variable or Option	Function
[*drive1:*][*path1*]*filename*	Specifies the drive, path, and name of the source files (that is, the files you want to replace or add to those in the destination directory). To specify multiple files, use wildcard characters in the *filename* parameter.
[*drive2:*]*path2*	Specifies the destination drive and directory where the source files should overwrite or be added to those already there.

/a	Adds new source files that do not already exist in the destination directory. You can't use this switch with the /s or /u switches.
/p	Tells DOS to prompt you for confirmation before replacing a file in the destination directory with a source file.
/r	Specifies that read-only files in the destination directory can be replaced.
/s	Specifies that files in all subdirectories of the destination directory be replaced.
/w	Pauses the REPLACE command until you press any key, giving you the opportunity to switch disks or insert a disk in the drive specified by the *drive1:* parameter.
/u	(Versions 4+) Specifies that DOS replace only those source files whose revision dates are more recent than those of their counterparts in the destination drive. (In versions prior to 4, you use /d instead of /u.)

Sample

Al in Finance has given you a floppy disk with all sorts of worksheet files on it. You want to copy only those files that are not already in your \123STUFF directory or that have a more recent revision date. To do this task, you first enter

```
replace a:\*.wk1 c:\123stuff /a
```

to have DOS copy only those files on Al's floppy disk that don't already exist in your \123STUFF directory. Next, you enter

```
replace a:\*.wk1 c:\123stuff /u /p
```

to have DOS replace only the more recent files from Al's floppy disk as well as to prompt you before replacing each one.

RESTORE

Restores files backed up with the BACKUP command (versions prior to Version 6).

DOSspeak

RESTORE *drive1:* *drive2:*[*path*[*filename*]] [/s] [/p]
[/b:*date*] [/a:*date*] [/e:*time*] [/l:*time*] [/m] [/n]
[d]

Variable or Option	Function
drive1:	Specifies the drive containing the floppy disk with the backup files.
drive2:[*path*[*filename*]]	Specifies the drive, directory, and name of the file(s) that will be restored. If you omit the *drive2:* parameter, DOS assumes you mean the current drive. If you include a *path* parameter, you must also include a *filename* parameter (which can include wildcard characters when specifying multiple files to be restored). The *path* parameter must match the directory from which the files were originally backed up.
/s	Specifies that files in all subdirectories of the destination directory be replaced.
/p	Tells DOS to prompt you for confirmation before restoring read-only files or files that have been revised since they were last backed up.
/b:*date*	Specifies that DOS restore only files modified on or before the *date* parameter (*mm-dd-yy* is the default format).
/a:*date*	Specifies that DOS restore only files modified on or after the *date* parameter (*mm-dd-yy* is the default format).
/e:*time*	Specifies that DOS restore only files modified at or before the *time* parameter (*hh:mm:ss* is the default format).
/l:*time*	Specifies that DOS restore only files modified at or later than the *time* parameter (*hh:mm:ss* is the default format).
/m	Specifies that DOS restore only those files that have been modified since they were backed up.
/n	Specifies that DOS restore only those files that have been deleted since they were backed up.

/d (Versions 5+) Specifies that DOS display the names of all the files on the backup disk that match the *filename* parameter, without actually restoring them.

Sample

You've backed up the files in your \123STUFF directory on a floppy disk and now, due to an unfortunate encounter with the DEL command, you need to restore all the files on the backup disk that are no longer in your \123STUFF directory. To do so, you put the backup disk in drive A and then enter

```
restore a:\*.* c:\123stuff /n
```

 See the example in *DOS For Dummies,* Chapter 19, section "Restoring using the pre-DOS 6 RESTORE command."

More stuff

If you used the MSBACKUP command in DOS 6, you can't use the RESTORE command to restore your backup files. Instead, you must use the Microsoft Backup program.

 See the example in *DOS For Dummies,* Chapter 19, section "Restoring using DOS 6's overrated MSBACKUP command."

SCANDISK

 Checks a disk for boo-boos and, if possible, fixes them. This nifty command can fix problems with the file allocation table (your so-called FAT table), file system structure (lost clusters and cross-linked files), directory tree, doublespace compression (see DBLSPACE), and the MS-DOS boot sector. In DOS 6.2, SCANDISK replaces the venerable CHKDSK command (you guys using earlier versions of DOS still need to rely on good old CHKDSK).

DOSspeak

To check and repair the current drive

```
SCANDISK
```

To check a noncurrent drive or all drives

```
SCANDISK [drive:[drive:...] | /ALL] [/CHECKONLY
| AUTOFIX [/NOSAVE] | /CUSTOM] [/SURFACE] [/
MONO] [/NOSUMMARY]
```

To check an unmounted Doublespace compressed drive

```
SCANDISK volume-name [/CHECKONLY | AUTOFIX
[/NOSAVE] | /CUSTOM] [/MONO] [/NOSUMMARY]
```

To check files for fragmentation

```
SCANDISK /FRAGMENT [drive:][path]filename
```

To undo repairs made previously with SCANDISK

```
SCANDISK /UNDO [undo-drive:] [/MONO]
```

Variable or Option	Function
[drive:][path]	Specifies the drive and directory to check and repair.
[drive:][path]filename	Specifies the drive, directory path, and file(s) to check for fragmentation. You can include the * and ? wildcard characters in the filename parameter to check all files whose names fit the general pattern.
volume-name	Specifies the name of the unmounted Doublespace volume that you want to check and repair.
undo-drive:	Specifies the drive containing the Undo disk so that you can undo repairs you just made with ScanDisk.
/ALL	Checks and repairs all local (actually attached) drives on your computer.
/CHECKONLY	Checks for errors on the specified drive(s) but does not attempt to repair any errors.
/AUTOFIX	Fixes errors that are located during checking without asking your permission (this is the default way of doing business for ScanDisk).
/NOSAVE	Deletes lost clusters located during the scan instead of saving them as files. This switch can only be used together with the /AUTOFIX switch. If you run ScanDisk with the /AUTOFIX switch but without the /NOSAVE switch, DOS saves the lost clusters as files in the root directory.
/CUSTOM	Runs ScanDisk using the configurations settings that are found in the CUSTOM

section of your SCANDISK.INI file (and you didn't even know you had one!).

/SURFACE Performs a surface scan of the specified drive(s). In scanning an uncompressed drive, ScanDisk lets you know that data can be reliably written and read from the disk. In scanning a compressed drive, ScanDisk lets you know that its data can be successfully uncompressed.

/MONO Tells ScanDisk to display the checking information for a monochrome monitor. Instead of wasting time setting this switch each time you use the SCANDISK command, you accomplish the same thing by putting the line DISPLAY=MONO in your SCANDISK.INI file (now that you know you have one).

/NOSUMMARY Stops ScanDisk from displaying a summary after checking each drive and stops Scan Disk from prompting you to supply an Undo disk when it finds errors.

Sample

Suppose that Al in Finance gives you a really lame-looking diskette and you want to know whether any of its data is still intact. To check this disk and fix any problems, put the disk in drive A and enter

```
SCANDISK A:
```

Suppose that you want to check your hard drive with ScanDisk without having any of the problems fixed. To do so when C: is the default directory, enter

```
SCANDISK /CHECKONLY
```

 See the examples in *DOS for Dummies*, Chapter 17, section "Scanning the Disk with SCANDISK" and Chapter 30, section "Commands You May Occasionally Use."

More stuff

You can't use the SCANDISK command to check a CD-ROM or Network drive nor to check a drive under the influence of the ASSIGN, JOIN, or SUBT commands or one created with the INTERLNK command. Also, don't try to use SCANDISK to check and repair a disk when other programs are running.

SET

Creates, deletes, or modifies the value assigned to a DOS environment variable.

DOSspeak

SET [*variable*=[*string*]]

Variable or Option	Function
variable	Specifies the name of the variable to create, edit, or delete.
string	Specifies the value to be assigned to your variable. To delete a variable, you omit the *string* parameter.

If you enter SET without any parameters, DOS lists the current values assigned to your environment variables.

Sample

Today, you need your directory listings to be sorted in descending date order (from the most recent to the least recent), with subdirectories preceding files. Rather than type `dir /o:g-d` each time, you assign the sorting switch that gives you the preferred order to the variable DIRCMD used by the DIR command (in Versions 5+). To do so, you enter

```
set dircmd=/o:g-d
```

Now, DOS automatically sorts the directory listings in your preferred order any time you use the DIR command during the current work session. If later you decide you want to return to the standard directory listing, you delete the DIRCMD variable by entering

```
set dircmd=
```

SETVER

Sets the version number that DOS reports to a particular program (available in Versions 5+).

DOSspeak

> **SETVER** [*drive:path*]*filename n.nn*

or

> **SETVER** [*drive:path*]*filename* [/delete [/quiet]]

Variable or Option	Function
[*drive:path*]	Specifies the drive and directory that contains the SETVER.EXE file that updates the table of applications. If you omit this parameter, DOS assumes current drive and directory.
filename	Specifies the name of the executable file that you want to add to the table of applications.
n.nn	Specifies the DOS version number that you want assigned to the file specified by the *filename* parameter in the table of applications.
/delete	Removes the file specified by the *filename* parameter from the table of applications. You can abbreviate this switch to /d.
/quiet	Suppresses the display of all messages when deleting a file (must be used with the /delete or /d switch).

If you enter SETVER without any parameters, DOS displays the contents of the table of applications.

More stuff

Note that assigning a new DOS version number to a program has no effect on the program's system requirements. If a particular program requires DOS 5 to run, using SETVER to set the DOS version number to 4.0 doesn't make the program run under this earlier version of DOS.

SHARE

Enables file-sharing and locking capabilities on a hard disk.

DOSspeak

> **SHARE** [/f:*space*] [/l:*locks*]

Variable or Option	Function
/f:*space*	Specifies how much memory (in bytes) to allocate for file-sharing information (the default is 2048).
/l:*locks*	Specifies how many files can be locked at one time (the default is 20).

If you enter SHARE without any parameters, DOS loads the Share program into memory by using the default values.

More stuff

This command is used in some network environments and with Windows.

SMARTDRV

Starts or configures the SMARTDrive program, which sets up a disk cache in extended memory for speeding up various disk operations (Version 6+).

DOSspeak

To start SMARTDrive and configure a disk cache from either your AUTOEXEX.BAT file or the DOS prompt:

```
[drive:] [path] SMARTDRV [/x] [[drive[+|-]]...]
[/u] [/c | /r] [/f | /n] [/l] [/v | /q | /s]
[initcachesize[wincachesize]]
[/e:elementsize] [/b:buffersize]
```

After SMARTDrive is running, to have the program write all cached information to a cached disk or to clear the contents of the existing cache and restart the program:

```
SMARTDRV [[drive[+ | -]]... [/c] [/r]
```

Variable or Option	Function
[*drive*:]*path*	Specifies the location of the SMARTDRV.EXE file. If you omit these parameters, DOS assumes that this file is in the search path (see PATH).
drive[+	-]	Specifies the letter of the disk(s) you want to cache. If you specify a drive without a plus or minus sign, DOS enables read-caching

	while disabling write-caching. If you add a plus sign, DOS enables both read- and write-caching for the specified drive. If you add a minus sign, DOS disables both read- and write-caching for the specified drive. If you omit the drive parameter, floppy disks created with Interlnk (see INTERLNK) are read-cached but not write-cached, while hard disk drives on your system are both read- and write-cached. To specify multiple drives, separate each drive letter with a space.
/e:*elementsize*	Specifies the amount of cache (in bytes) that SMARTDrive moves at a time. The *elementsize* parameter can be any of the following values: 1024, 2048, 4096, or 8192 (the default).
initcachesize	Specifies the size of the cache (in kilobytes) when SMARTDrive starts and Windows isn't running. If you omit this parameter, SMARTDrive sets the value according to how much memory your computer has (see the following table).
wincachesize	Specifies how much SMARTDrive reduces the cache size (in kilobytes) to recover memory necessary for running Windows. If you omit this parameter, SMARTDrive sets the value according to how much memory your computer has (see the following table). If you specify an *initcachesize* parameter that is smaller than the *wincachesize* parameter, DOS sets the *initcachesize* to the *wincachesize*.
/b:*buffersize*	Specifies the size of the read-ahead buffer. The *buffersize* parameter can be set to any multiple of the *elementsize* parameter.
/c	Writes all cached information to the appropriate cached disk. Use this option prior to turning off your computer to ensure that all cached information is saved on disk (you need not use this switch before rebooting with Ctrl-Alt-Del, only prior to manually shutting down or pressing the Reset button).
/r	Clears the contents of the existing cache and restarts SMARTDrive.

/l	Prevents SMARTDrive from automatically loading into the upper memory blocks (UMBs) even when these blocks are available.
/q	Instructs SMARTDrive not to display status messages when the program starts (only if the program encounters an error when starting). You can't use this switch with the /v switch.
/v	Instructs SMARTDrive to display status messages along with error messages when it starts. You can't use this switch with the /q switch.
/s	Displays additional information about the status of SMARTDrive.
/x	Disables the write-behind caching on all new drives.
/u	Instructs SMARTDRV not to load the CD-ROM caching module even, if you have a CD-ROM drive.
/f	Causes SMARTDrive to write the cached data after each command completes (the default mode).
/n	Instructs SMARTDrive to write the cached data when the system is idle.

The following table shows the default values for the *initcachesize* and *wincachesize* parameters, depending on the amount of extended memory.

Extended Memory	Default initcachesize	Default wincachesize
Up to 1M	All extended memory	Zero (no caching)
Up to 2M	1M	256K
Up to 4M	1M	512K
Up to 6M	2M	1M
Over 6M	2M	2M

If you enter SMARTDrive without any parameters, DOS sets up a disk cache using the default values.

Sample

To set up a disk cache with the default size of 1MB on a computer that has 2MB of extended memory total each time you start your computer, you add the following command to your AUTOEXEC.BAT file:

```
c:\dos\smartdrv
```

To ensure that cached information is saved on disk before you shut down your computer, at the DOS prompt, you enter

```
smartdrv /c
```

More stuff

Don't use the SMARTDRV command after you've started Windows. For SMARTDrive to use extended memory, your CONFIG.SYS file must contain a DEVICE command that loads the HIMEM.SYS driver or another driver that manages extended memory. Also, to do double buffering that provides compatibility for hard-disk controllers that can't work with the memory provided by EMM386 device driver or Windows running in 386-enhanced mode, you need to add a DEVICE command to your CONFIG.SYS file that loads the SMARTDRV.EXE. See DEVICE in the Configuration Commands section for details.

SORT

Sorts lines of text and writes the results to the screen, a file, or another device.

DOSspeak

SORT [/r] [/+n] < [drive1:][*path1*]*filename1*
[> [*drive2:*][*path*]*filename2*]

or

[*command* |] **SORT** [/r] [/+*n*]
[*drive2:*][*path*]*filename2*]

Variable or Option	Function
/r	Reverses the normal sort order (A to Z; then 0 to 9 — called ascending order) to Z to A; then 9 to 0 (called descending).

/+n	Sorts the lines by the characters in the number of the column specified by the *n* parameter. If you omit this switch, DOS sorts the text according to the characters in the first column.
[*drive1:*][*path1*]*filename1*	Specifies the drive, directory, and name of the file to be sorted.
[*drive2:*][*path*]*filename2*	Specifies the drive, directory, and name of the file where the sorted output is to be saved.
command	Specifies the DOS command whose output is to be sorted.

If you enter the SORT command without any parameters, DOS sorts the lines of text that you type at the keyboard (each line separated by a carriage return) according to the character in the first column, as soon as you press Ctrl-Z or F6 and press Enter.

Sample

To sort a list of CEOs for client companies saved in a file called CEOS.TXT in your \MYTURF directory by the first character of their names and store the sorted names in a file called CEOSORT.TXT on a disk in drive A, you enter

```
sort \myturf\ceos.txt a:\ceosort.txt
```

To sort the output of a directory listing in descending order by filename, you enter

```
dir | sort /r
```

SUBST

Associates a drive letter with a directory, making the directory into what's known as a *virtual drive* (as opposed to a real, physical drive on your computer, such as A or C).

DOSspeak

```
SUBST [drive1: [drive2:]path]
```

or

```
SUBST drive1: /d
```

Variable or Option	Function
drive1:	Specifies the letter of the virtual drive that you want to assign to the specified directory.
[drive2:]path	Specifies the physical drive and directory that is to be assigned to the virtual drive.
/d	Deletes the virtual drive specified by the *drive1:* parameter.

If you enter SUBST without any other parameters, DOS displays a list of all virtual drives currently assigned.

Sample

To be able to refer to your \MYTURF directory on drive C as drive D, you enter

```
subst d: c:\myturf
```

Then, to check the status of your new virtual drive D, you enter

```
subst
```

and DOS displays the current substitution status as

```
D: => C:\MYTURF
```

When you're ready to delete this virtual drive, you enter

```
subst d: /d
```

More stuff

You can't use the SUBST command on a drive under the influence of any of the following DOS commands: ASSIGN, BACKUP, CHKDISK, DISKCOMP, DISKCOPY, FASTOPEN, FDISK, FORMAT, LABEL, RECOVER, RESTORE, or SYS.

SYS

Transfers the DOS system files to a specified disk so that you can boot your computer with that disk.

DOSspeak

SYS [*drive1:*][*path*] *drive2:*

Variable or Option	Function
drive1:[*path*]	Specifies the drive and directory containing the DOS system files. In Versions 4+, if you omit these parameters, DOS assumes that you mean the current directory.
drive2:	Specifies the drive containing the disk onto which you want to copy the system files. This disk must be formatted but have no files on it.

Sample

You just formatted a floppy disk in drive A but forgot to use the /s switch to copy the system files onto it so that in an emergency (that is, when DOS can't find your hard disk), you could use it to boot the computer. To copy the system files, you enter

```
sys c: a:
```

After copying these files, you use the COPY command to copy the COMMAND.COM file to the floppy disk in drive A (this step is unnecessary in DOS 5 and later versions).

TIME

Displays and changes the current time used by DOS and application programs to add the time stamp to files.

DOSspeak

TIME [*hh:mm*[:*ss*[.*xx*]]] [a | p]

Variable or Option	Function
hh	Specifies the hours based in a 24-hour clock (0 to 23, where 0 represents 12 midnight).
:*mm*	Specifies the minutes (between 0 and 59). If you omit the :*mm* parameter, DOS uses 0 minutes.
:*ss*	Specifies the number of seconds (between 0 and 59). If you omit the :*ss* parameter, DOS uses 0 seconds.
.*xx*	Specifies the hundredths of seconds (between 0 and 99). If you omit the .*xx* parameter, DOS uses 0 hundredths.

a | p   (Versions 5+) Specifies a.m. or p.m. when
                               using a COUNTRY code whose date format
                               supports a 12-hour clock (as does the U.S.
                               default).

Enter TIME without any parameters to display the current time
setting.

Sample

It's Monday morning right after you've changed all the clocks at
home to Daylight Savings Time. To see what time your computer
thinks it is, you enter

```
time
```

and press Enter. According to your watch, it's now 10:30 a.m., but
your computer still thinks it's 9:30 a.m. To get your computer's
clock up to date, you enter

```
time 10:30
```

 See the example in *DOS For Dummies,* Chapter 6, section "The
Date and Time."

TREE

Displays a diagram showing the directory structure of the
specified disk or path.

DOSspeak

TREE [*drive:*][*path*] [/f] [/a]

Variable or Option	Function
drive:	Specifies the drive whose directory structure is to be displayed. If you omit the *drive:* parameter, DOS assumes current drive.
path	Specifies the topmost directory to be included in the diagram. If you omit the *path* parameter, DOS displays the entire directory structure of the disk specified by the *drive:* parameter.
/f	Displays the name of each file in the directory included in the diagram.
/a	Displays the diagram with text (ASCII) characters rather than with graphics

characters (which your printer may not be able to reproduce).

If you enter TREE without any parameters, DOS displays the directory structure of the current drive starting with the current directory.

Sample

You need to figure out in which directory Sue keeps her 1-2-3 worksheet files because she's home sick and you're stuck doing her spreadsheets today. To display the directory structure of her hard disk one screenful at a time, you enter

```
tree c: | more
```

After examining the structure (and locating the whereabouts of her worksheet files C:\123\SUESHEET), you decide it would be good to have a printout of this diagram for later reference. Because Sue's old printer doesn't support graphics characters, you need to turn off the graphics when you print this diagram by entering

```
tree c: /a > prn
```

See the example in *DOS For Dummies,* Chapter 16, section "The Tree Structure."

TYPE

Displays the contents of a text file on your screen.

DOSspeak

TYPE [*drive:*][*path*]*filename*

Variable or Option	Function
[*drive:*]*path*	Specifies the drive and directory containing the file whose contents you want displayed. If you omit the drive and path, DOS assumes that the file is in the current drive and directory.
filename	Specifies the name of the text file whose contents you want displayed.

Sample

You've just gotten a new program that contains a READ.ME text file on the first disk. To see if it contains anything that you should pay any attention to, you display its text on-screen by entering

```
type a:read.me
```

Unfortunately, a whole bunch of warnings and stuff like that fly by in a blur that you can't possibly read. So this time, you display the file a screenful at a time by entering

```
type a:read.me | more
```

See the example in *DOS For Dummies,* Chapter 1, section "Looking at Files."

More stuff

If you use the TYPE command in attempting to display a nontext file (like a 1-2-3 worksheet or something like that), instead of numbers and stuff you can read, strange hieroglyphics appear, accompanied by spasmodic beeps. If these events happen, don't worry, you haven't screwed up the file or anything like that; the signals just mean that the file's information is stored in some sort of binary format that invariably gives the TYPE command indigestion.

UNDELETE

Restores files deleted by mistake with the DEL or ERASE command (available in Versions 5+ only).

DOSspeak

```
UNDELETE [drive:][path][filename] [/dt | /ds |dos]
```

or

```
UNDELETE [/list | /all | /purge[drive] | status
  | /load | /unload | /s[drive] | /t[drive][-entries
```

Variable or Option	Function
[*drive:*][*path*]*filename*	Specifies the disk, directory, and name of the file(s) that you want to undelete. To undelete multiple files, use wildcard characters in the *filename* parameter.
/list	Lists all the files that you can undelete without prompting you to undelete them.
/all	Undeletes all specified files without prompting you.

/dt	Undeletes only files included in the deletion-tracking file produced by the MIRROR command (the default when a deletion-tracking file exists).
/dos	Undeletes only files listed as deleted by DOS (the default when a deletion-tracking file doesn't exist).
/ds	(Version 6) Recovers files protected by Delete Sentry.
/purge[*drive*]	(Version 6) Purges all files in the Delete Sentry directory.
/status	(Version 6) Displays the protection method in effect for each drive.
/load	(Version 6) Loads the Undelete memory-resident program.
/unload	(Version 6) Unloads the Undelete memory-resident program.
/s[*drive*]	(Version 6) Enables the Delete Sentry method of protection and loads the memory-resident portion of the Undelete program. The *drive* parameter specifies the drive where DOS records the recovery information. If you omit the *drive* parameter, DOS assumes you mean the current drive.
/t*drive*	(Version 6) Loads the deletion-tracking program for the *drive* specified after the /t switch. This program saves information each time you delete a file in the specified *drive* in a special file called PCTRACKR.DEL, which is located in the root directory of the *drive*.
-*entries*	(Version 6) Specifies the number of entries the deletion-tracking program will save. Default values for the -*entries* parameter vary according to the size of the disk specified by the *drive* parameter (see the table in the MIRROR entry).

If you enter UNDELETE without any parameters, DOS lists those files in the current drive and directory that can be undeleted and prompts you to undelete each one.

Sample

The moment you press Enter, it hits you that instead of deleting the obsolete version of a file, you just eighty-sixed the version you spent the last two hours editing (you should have typed the filename BIGDOC1.TXT but entered BIGDOC2.TXT instead). To get this deleted file back and avoid having to redo all the work, you enter

```
undelete bigdoc1.txt
```

DOS then displays the name of the file as

```
?IGDOC2 TXT
```

and prompts you to undelete it. When you press Y, DOS next prompts you to type the first character of the filename. After pressing B and then Enter, you see that wonderfully reassuring message `File successfully undeleted` right above the now beautiful DOS prompt.

See the example in *DOS For Dummies,* Chapter 3, section "Undeleting a File."

More stuff

Be sure to use the UNDELETE command as soon as you discover that you blew off a file by mistake. If you continue to work (especially when moving and copying other files around), DOS may use the deleted file's space for other files, making it impossible for this command to work its magic.

UNFORMAT

Rebuilds the directory structure and restores the files on a disk that was erased with the FORMAT command (available in Versions 5+).

DOSspeak

UNFORMAT *drive:* [/u] [/l] [/test] [/p]

or

UNFORMAT *drive:* [/j]

or

UNFORMAT /partn [/l]

Variable or Option	Function
drive:	Specifies the disk whose contents you want to rebuild.
/j	(Version 5 only) Compares the contents of files created by the MIRROR command with the system information without rebuilding the structure or restoring the files.
/u	(Version 5 only) Rebuilds the directory structure and restores the files on the specified disk without using the file information recorded with the MIRROR command.
/l	Lists all the file and directory names on the specified disk and then prompts you to use this information to rebuild the disk. When used with the /partn switch, DOS displays the partition table of a hard disk but does not rebuild the disk.
/test	Lists all the file and directory names on the specified disk but does not rebuild the disk.
/p	Sends the UNFORMAT messages to the printer connected to LPT1.
/partn	(Version 5 only) Restores the partition tables of a hard disk, provided that you don't use this switch with /l and that DOS finds the PARTNSAV.FIL created with the MIRROR command's /partn switch.

Sample

Your very agitated Boss comes to you looking for an unlabeled high-density disk that was "right there on the desk" earlier this morning. According to the Boss, this disk contains the only copies of the budget worksheet files that the president of the company wants right after lunch today. Suddenly, you realize that the unmarked high-density disk that you "borrowed" from the Boss's office earlier and just finished FORMATTING is the one that's "lost!" In an attempt to resuscitate the Boss's trashed budget files and save your job, you put the newly formatted (but still empty) disk in drive A and enter

```
unformat a:
```

Fortunately for all (especially you because you really need this job), your Boss wisely saved the budget worksheets in a subdirectory called \WHATIF and the UNFORMAT command is able to completely rebuild this directory and everything in it.

See the example in *DOS For Dummies,* Chapter 19, section "I Just Reformatted My Disk."

More stuff

UNFORMAT can't restore a disk that has been formatted with the FORMAT command's /u (unconditional) switch, nor can it restore a network drive. Keep in mind that you need to use UNFORMAT to restore the data on a disk before you put any files on the newly (and mistakenly) formatted disk. Also be aware that UNFORMAT is best at rebuilding subdirectories and restoring their files (files in the root directory of the disk are often irretrievable) and that this command is much more successful with a disk containing file and directory information recorded with the MIRROR command.

VER

Displays the version of DOS you're running on your computer.

DOSspeak

```
ver
```

Sample

Today, you're using Cindy's computer. However, you don't remember what version of DOS she has on her machine (and you want to make sure that she has at least Version 5, with the UNDELETE and UNFORMAT commands, before you mess with any of her files). To find out what the DOS version is, you enter

```
ver
```

See the example in *DOS For Dummies,* Chapter 2, section "Names and Versions."

VERIFY

Turns on or off the switch that controls disk-write verification used with commands like COPY and DISKCOPY to check whether data was written correctly on a disk.

DOSspeak

VERIFY [on | off]

where the on parameter turns on disk-write verification and the off parameter turns off disk-write verification. If you enter VERIFY without one of these parameters, DOS displays the current disk-write verification (the default is off).

Sample

To turn on disk-write verification before you begin copying a bunch of files, you enter

```
verify on
```

Then, later in the day, to verify that disk-write verification is still on before you do more copying, you enter

```
verify
```

More stuff

You can also turn on disk-write verification by adding the /v switch when you are using the COPY or DISKCOPY command.

VOL

Displays the current volume label and serial number assigned to a specified disk.

DOSspeak

VOL ⌊*drive:*⌋

where *drive:* specifies the disk for which you want the volume label. If you omit the *drive:* parameter, DOS displays the volume label of the current drive.

Sample

You're looking for a high-density floppy disk with the volume label VITAL STUFF. To see if the unlabeled disk you just picked out of a heap on your desk is the one you want, you put the disk in drive A and enter

```
vol a:
```

Unfortunately, this disk proves not to be the one you're looking for; its volume label is PETTY STUFF. Better luck next disk!

See the example in *DOS For Dummies,* Chapter 12, section "Changing the Volume Label."

More stuff

For information on how to add, change, or delete a volume label, see LABEL.

VSAFE

Continuously monitors your computer for any nasty computer viruses and displays a warning should one be detected (available in DOS 6+ only).

DOSspeak

VSAFE [/*option*[+ | -]...] [/ne] [/nx]
[/A*x* | /C*x*] [/n] [/d] [/u]

Variable or Option	Function
/*option*[+ | -]	Specifies how DOS monitors for viruses (see the following table for possible values). To turn on an option, follow the option value with a + (plus). To turn off an option, follow the option value with a - (minus or hyphen). To specify mulitple /*option* parameters, separate each one with a space.
/ne	Prevents DOS from loading VSAFE into expanded RAM memory.
/nx	Prevents DOS from loading VSAFE into extended RAM memory.
/A*x*	Sets Alt plus the letter you specify for the *x* parameter as the hot keys that display the VSAFE screen.
/C*x*	Sets Ctrl plus the letter you specify for the *x* parameter as the hot keys that display the VSAFE screen.
/n	Enables VSAFE to check for viruses on network drives.
/d	Turns off checksumming.
/u	Removes VSAFE from memory.

The VSAFE /*option* parameters can include any of the following:

USAFE Options	Function
1	Warns of formatting that could completely erase the hard disk (the default is on).

2	Warns of an attempt by the program to remain in memory (the default is off).
3	Prevents programs from writing to disk (the default is off).
4	Checks the executable files that DOS opens (the default is on).
5	Checks all disks for boot sector viruses (the default is on).
6	Warns of attempts to write to the boot sector or partition of a hard disk (the default is on).
7	Warns of attempts to write to the boot sector of a floppy disk (the default is off).
8	Warns of attempts to modify executable files (the default is off).

If you enter VSAFE without any parameters, DOS loads the VSAFE program using the default values.

Sample

Al in Finance just called to let you know that Sue's computer picked up such a bad virus that they couldn't save any of the data on her hard disk. Now that you've got DOS 6 on your system, you decide it's time to monitor your computer for viruses. To turn on virus monitoring and make Alt-V the VSAFE hot keys, you enter

```
vsafe /Av
```

More stuff

VSAFE is a terminate-and-stay-resident (TSR) program that uses about 22K of memory.

Don't use the VSAFE command when you are running Microsoft Windows on your computer.

XCOPY

Selectively copies files, including the files in subdirectories if you want to include them.

DOSspeak

XCOPY *source* [*destination*] [/a | /m] [/d:*date*]
[/p] [/s [/e]] [/v] [/w] [/-y] [/y]

Variable or Option	Function
source	Specifies the drive, directory, and name of the source files (that is, the ones to copy). If you specify only a drive, DOS copies all the files in the specified drive. If you specify a path without a filename, DOS copies all the files in the specified directory of the current drive. To copy multiple files, use wildcard characters when specifying the filename.
destination	Specifies the drive, directory, and/or new names of the destination files. If you omit the *destination* parameter, DOS assumes you mean the current drive and directory and does not rename the copied files.
/a	Copies source files that have their archive attributes set, without modifying the attribute (see ATTRIB for more info).
/m	Copies source files that have their archive attributes set; then turns off the archive attribute in the *source* files (see ATTRIB for more info).
/d:*date*	Copies source files that have been modified on or after the date specified by the *date* parameter (*mm-dd-yy* is the default format).
/p	Prompts you before creating each destination file.
/s	Copies files in directories and subdirectories unless they are empty.
/e	Copies subdirectories even if they are empty.
/v	Verifies each file as it is written.
/w	Prompts you to press a key before starting the copying process (giving you time to switch disks).
/-y	Forces XCOPY to prompt you before overwriting an existing file.
/y	Allows XCOPY to overwrite existing files without prompting.

Sample

Al in Finance needs a copy of all the files in your \MYTURF directory, including those in the \STUFF and \NONSENSE subdirectories that have been created or modified since February 15, 1993. To make these copies, you enter

Section II:
Batch Commands

A *batch file* (or *batch program*) is a collection of DOS commands saved in a text file with the BAT extension. When you type the filename at the DOS prompt, DOS executes each command in the batch file — as if you typed them in manually. The most famous batch file in DOS is the AUTOEXEC.BAT file.

You can create or edit batch files with the DOS Editor if you're running Version 5 or later (see EDIT in the DOS Commands sections). Pray that you have DOS 5+. If you're using an earlier version of DOS and you're desperate, you can use Edlin, the terrible DOS line editor.

When you edit a batch file, you enter each DOS command on its own line of the file. Type them in the order in which you want the commands played back. If you use a word processor, remember that you have to save your batch file with a BAT extension in a text file format (don't save a batch file in the word processor's regular format or it won't run).

When creating a batch file, you can use any DOS command that you would normally type at the command prompt. In addition, you can include the special batch file commands included in this section, as appropriate.

The full topic of "Batch File Programming" is best left to books specific to that subject. For now, you may want to have your DOS guru show you a few tricks, or you may just stare slack-jawed in awe of this potentially fun aspect of DOS.

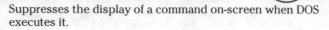

@

Suppresses the display of a command on-screen when DOS executes it.

DOSspeak

> @*command*

where *command* is the DOS command that you don't want displayed.

CALL

Calls one batch program from another without causing the first one to stop. When DOS finishes executing all the commands in the second batch program, it returns to the first program. Then DOS executes the first command under the CALL command that was just executed.

DOSspeak

> CALL [*drive:*][*path*]**filename** [*batch-parameters*]

Variable or Option	Function
[*drive:*][*path*]*filename*	Specifies the drive, directory, and name of the batch file you're calling. This *filename* parameter must have a BAT extension.
batch-parameters	Specifies any arguments required by a batch file that contains replaceable parameters.

CHOICE

Prompts you to make a choice in a batch program. You can then branch the batch program depending upon what choice you make (available in DOS 6+ only).

DOSspeak

> CHOICE [/c[:]*keys*] [/n] [/s] [/t[:]*c,nn*] [*text*]

Variable or Option	Function
/c[:]*keys*	Specifies which keys are presented as choices in the prompt. When the CHOICE command is executed, the specified keys appear in brackets separated by commas and terminated with a question mark — for example, [A,B,C]? when you enter /c:abc. If you omit the /c switch, DOS displays [Y,N]? as the default choice.
/n	Suppresses the CHOICE prompt and displays only the message that precedes this prompt (specified by the *text* parameter).
/s	Makes the CHOICE command case sensitive. When the /s switch is not used, both lower- and uppercase letters are accepted as matches to the *keys* parameters.
/t[:]*c,nn*	Specifies a default key and how long CHOICE is to wait before defaulting to that key. The *c* parameter specifies the default key (it must, however, be one of those specified with the /c switch). The *nn* parameter specifies the number of seconds to pause (between 0 and 99).
text	Specifies the message you want displayed in front of the CHOICE prompt created with the /c switch. You only need to enclose this text in quotation marks when the text contains the / (forward slash) character. If you omit the *text* parameter, CHOICE displays only the prompt specified with the /c switch.

Sample

To prompt the user to choose between terminating the batch file or continuing, you enter

```
choice /c:qc Quit now, or Continue processing?
```

When you run the batch file with this CHOICE command, on-screen you see

```
Quit now, or Continue processing? [Q,C]?
```

ECHO

Controls whether DOS displays commands in a batch file as it executes them. You can also use ECHO to display your own messages to the user.

DOSspeak

ECHO [on | off]

or

ECHO [*message*]

Variable or Option	*Function*
on	Turns on ECHO so that DOS commands are displayed as executed (the default setting).
off	Turns off ECHO so that DOS commands are not displayed as executed.
message	Specifies the message you want the user to see even when ECHO is turned off. To insert a blank line in the display with ECHO, type a period with no space after ECHO.

If you enter ECHO without any parameters, DOS tells you whether ECHO is currently on or off.

FOR

Runs a specified DOS command for each file in a set of files.

DOSspeak

FOR %%*variable* **in (***set***) do** *command*
[*command-parameters*]

Variable or Option	*Function*
%%*variable*	Specifies the name of the variable that you want DOS to assign each item, in turn, in the *set* parameter. When specifying the variable, don't use numbers between 0 and 9 because DOS will confuse these numbers with command line replaceable parameters.

set	Specifies the files, replaceable parameters representing filenames, or text strings that are assigned in sequence to the %%*variable* and then processed by the specified *command*. Each file or string in a set must be separated by a space, and all the items in the entire set must be enclosed in parentheses. When specifying items in the set, you can use wildcard characters.
command	Specifies the DOS command you want executed (which can be any command other than the FOR command).
command-parameters	Specifies any parameters or switches used by the specified command, including the FOR command's %%*variable* and command line replaceable parameters (%0 through %9).

Sample

To have your batch command delete all files with JNK and BAK extensions in your \MYTURF directory, you enter

```
for %%ext in (\myturf\*.jnk \myturf\*.bak) do
del %%ext
```

GOTO

Redirects execution in the batch file to a line identified with a particular label.

DOSspeak

GOTO *label*

where *label* is the name of the line in the batch file at which execution is to resume. When you label the line in the batch file, the label name must appear alone preceded by a colon.

Sample

To identify the commands on the last two lines of the batch file with the label End, you enter

```
:End
```

on its own line right above the lines with the last two commands. Then, at the place in the batch file where you want execution to jump to these last two commands, you enter

```
goto End
```

IF

Performs conditional processing in the batch program. If the condition in the IF command is true, DOS carries out the specified command. Otherwise, DOS ignores the command.

DOSspeak

```
IF [not] errorlevel number command
```

or

```
IF [not] string1==string2 command
```

or

```
IF [not] exist filename command
```

Variable or Option	Function
not	Specifies that DOS should carry out the specified command only when the condition is not true (that is, the condition is false).
errorlevel *number*	Specifies a true condition when the previous program executed by COMMAND.COM returned an exit code equal to or greater than the value specified by the *number* parameter.
command	Specifies the DOS command to carry out when the condition is true.
string1==string2	Specifies a true condition when *string1* and *string2* are the same (including case). These *string1* and *string2* parameters can be replaceable parameters (such as %0) or literal strings (such as bigdoc.txt). Literal strings do not have to be enclosed in quotation marks.
exist *filename*	Specifies a true condition when DOS locates the file specified by the *filename* parameter.

Sample

To tell the batch file to jump to the section at the bottom of the file labeled End and execute the commands it finds there if DOS can't locate your BIGDOC.TXT file in your \MYTURF directory, you enter

```
if not exist c:\myturf\bigdoc.txt goto End
```

To display an error message on-screen when this file is not found, you enter instead

```
if not exist c:\myturf\bigdoc.txt echo This
file's no longer in \MYTURF!
```

PAUSE

Pauses the execution of the batch file until the user presses a key. Optionally, displays your message on-screen while the batch file is paused.

DOSspeak

PAUSE [*message*]

where *message* is the text of the message you want displayed while the program is paused. Note that the user sees the *message* only when ECHO is on. Whether you enter PAUSE alone or with a *message* parameter, DOS always displays its own user message during the pause (even when ECHO is off).

REM

Lets you add comments to your batch file that will be displayed when ECHO is on (the default).

DOSspeak

REM [*string*]

where *string* is the text of the comments you want to add to the batch file.

More stuff

If you don't want your comments displayed, precede the REM command with the @ command or, better yet, turn ECHO off with @echo off at the top of the batch file.

SHIFT

Modifies the position of the replaceable parameters in a batch program by discarding the %0 parameter and then moving each subsequent parameter to a lower number (%1 to %0, %2 to %1, and so on).

DOSspeak

```
SHIFT
```

More stuff

The SHIFT command lets you specify more than ten replaceable parameters (%0 to %9) in the command line. Use SHIFT as often as you need it to process all the command arguments. Just keep in mind that each time you use SHIFT, DOS discards the %0 replaceable parameter.

Section III:
Configuration Commands

The DOS commands that you enter at the DOS prompt or put into a batch file tell DOS to do something specific like delete a file or format a disk. Configuration commands tell DOS how your system is put together so that the application programs you run can take advantage of the particular memory arrangement or hardware devices attached to your computer.

Unlike standard DOS commands that you can enter at the DOS prompt, configuration commands are always placed in a special file — CONFIG.SYS (pronounced *config-dot-sis*). This file is read into your computer's memory the first thing each time you start your PC. Because the CONFIG.SYS file, like the AUTOEXEC.BAT file, is used each time you start the computer, you need to make sure that this file is located in the root directory of the drive from which your computer boots, meaning drive C.

Like the AUTOEXEC.BAT file, the CONFIG.SYS file is a text file containing a list of commands that DOS is to execute when you boot the computer. Because it consists of text, you can edit this file with any word processor that deals with text files, the DOS Editor (the EDIT command in Version 5), or EDLIN. Ugh, EDLIN.

When editing your CONFIG.SYS file, you can include any of the configuration commands covered in this section.

BREAK

Tells DOS how often to check for the Ctrl-C or Ctrl-Break keys used to terminate a program or batch files prematurely.

DOSspeak

BREAK=[on | off]

Variable or Option	Function
on	Turns on extended Ctrl-C checking so that DOS checks during read and write operations as well as when it reads from the keyboard or writes to the screen or a printer.
off	Turns off extended Ctrl-C checking.

BUFFERS

Allocates memory for a number of disk buffers when you start your computer.

DOSspeak

BUFFERS=n[, *m*]

Variable or Option	Function
n	Specifies the number of disk buffers (between 1 and 99).
m	Specifies the number of buffers in the secondary buffer cache (between 1 and 8).

More stuff

In versions prior to 3.3, DOS uses 2 as the default number of buffers. In Versions 3.3+, the number depends on how your system is configured (with 15 being the default on a computer with 512K or more RAM).

COUNTRY

Configures DOS to recognize the character set, the sort order, and the punctuation, date, time, and currency conventions for a particular country.

DOSspeak

COUNTRY=*xxx*[,[*yyy*][,[***drive:***][*path*]*filename*]]

Variable or Option	Function
xxx	Specifies the COUNTRY code. The *xxx* parameter is a three-digit number, corresponding to the international dialing prefix of the country, including any leading zeros necessary to make up three digits.
yyy	Specifies the code page, which in turn specifies the character set to use (see the table in the KEYB entry in the DOS Commands section).
[*drive:*][*path*]*filename*	Specifies the drive, directory, and name of the file containing the country information. If you omit the *drive:* and *path* parameters, DOS assumes the file is in the search directory (see PATH in the DOS Commands section). If you omit the *filename* parameter as well, DOS uses the COUNTRY.SYS file.

Sample

To enable Cousin Olaf to use the Norwegian keyboard, sort order, dates and times, and the whole Nordic ten yards on your computer, you add

```
country=047,865
```

to your CONFIG.SYS file.

DEVICE

Loads a particular device driver into memory so that your computer can use that device.

DOSspeak

DEVICE=[*drive:*][*path*]***filename*** [*dd-parameters*]

Variable or Option	Function
[*drive:*][*path*]*filename*	Specifies the drive, directory, and name of the device driver file. If you omit the *drive:* and *path* parameters, DOS assumes that the driver file is on the disk and directory used to boot the computer.
dd-parameters	Specifies any command line information required by the device driver.

More stuff

When you have multiple devices to specify, you enter multiple DEVICE commands in your CONFIG.SYS file. Be aware, however, that the order in which these devices are loaded can be critical — so check your documentation for details. The standard device drivers in DOS 6 include ANSI.SYS, DISPLAY.SYS, DRIVER.SYS, DBLSPACE.SYS, EGA.SYS, EMM386.EXE, HIMEM.SYS, INTERLNK.EXE, POWER.EXE, RAMDRIVE.SYS, SETVER.EXE, and SMARTDRV.SYS. For specific information on any of these device drivers, at the DOS prompt, type help followed by the device driver filename, for example

```
help interlnk.exe
```

DEVICEHIGH

Loads a particular device driver into the upper memory of your 386 or 486 computer, freeing more conventional memory for your application programs.

DOSspeak

DEVICEHIGH=[*drive:*][*path*]***filename*** [*dd-parameters*]

or

DEVICEHIGH=[/ l : *region1*[, *minsize1*][; *region2*[*minsize2*]
[/ s]]=[*drive:*][*path*]**filename** [*dd-parameters*]

Variable or Option	Function
[*drive:*][*path*]*filename*	Specifies the drive, directory, and name of the device driver file you want to load into upper memory. If you omit the *drive:* and *path* parameters, DOS assumes that the driver file is on the disk and directory used to boot the computer. By default, DOS loads the driver into the largest free upper memory block (UMB) and makes all other UMBs available for the driver's use.
dd-parameters	Specifies any command line information required by the device driver.
/l:*region1*[,*minsize1*] [;*region2*[,*minsize2*]	Specifies one or more regions of memory in which the device driver is to be loaded. To ensure that a driver won't be loaded into a region that's too small for it, you can also specify the *minsize* parameter for the particular *region* parameter that you specify.
/s	Normally used by the MemMaker program to shrink the UMB (upper memory block) to its minimum size while the device drive is loading. Don't use this /s switch unless you're certain that shrinking the UMB won't interfere with loading the device driver. You can only use the /s switch with the /l switch, and when you've specified both a *region* and *minsize* parameter.

More stuff

To find out how a particular device driver uses memory, enter the
MEM command with the /m switch and the device driver's
filename. Also, your CONFIG.SYS file must contain the following
commands to make the upper memory area available for loading
device drivers before you use the DEVICEHIGH command:

```
device=c:\dos\himem.sys
device=c:\dos\emm386.exe ram
dos=umb
```

DOS

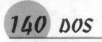

Enables DOS to load part of itself into the High Memory Area (HMA) and/or maintain a link with the upper memory blocks (UMBs) of reserved memory (available with Versions 5+).

DOSspeak

```
DOS=high | low[,umb |,noumb]
```

or

```
DOS=[high, | low,]umb | noumb
```

Variable or Option	Function
high	Causes DOS to load part of itself into the HMA.
low	Causes DOS to load itself into conventional memory (the default).
umb	Causes DOS to establish a link to the UMBs in reserved memory that can be used by the LOADHIGH DOS command or DEVICEHIGH configuration command.
noumb	Causes DOS not to establish a link with reserved memory.

More stuff

You must load the device driver HIMEM.SYS or some other extended memory manager before you configure DOS to UMB or HIGH.

DRIVPARM

Defines parameters for devices like disk and tape drives when you start your computer.

DOSspeak

```
DRIVEPARM=/d:number [/c] [/f:factor] [/h:heads]
[/i] [/n] [/s:sectors] [t:tracks]
```

Variable or Option	Function
/d:*number*	Specifies the number of a physical drive between 0 and 255, where 0 = drive A, 1 = drive B, 2 = drive C, and so on.
/c	Specifies that the drive can detect when the door is closed.
/f:*factor*	Specifies the drive type. The factor parameter can be any of the following: 0 (for 160/180K or 320/360K, 5¼-inch), 1 (for 1.2M, 5¼-inch), 2 (for 720K, 3½-inch), 5 (for a hard disk), 6 (for a tape backup), 7 (for 1.44M, 3½-inch), 8 (for a read/write optical disk), or 9 (for 2.88M, 3½-inch).
/h:*heads*	Specifies the maximum number of heads (between 1 through 99).
/i	(Versions 4+) Specifies that the drive is an electronically compatible 3½-inch floppy drive (that is, one that uses your existing floppy-disk-drive controller).
/n	Specifies that the drive is nonremovable.
/s:*sectors*	Specifies the number of sectors per track (between 1 through 99).
/t:*tracks*	Specifies the number of tracks per side (between 1 through 999).

More stuff

You can include multiple DRIVPARM commands in your CONFIG.SYS, each one defining the characteristics of a particular floppy or tape drive in your system.

FCBS (File Control Blocks)

Specifies the number of file control blocks (FCBs) that DOS can open at one time (in case you care, FCBs are data structures that reside in an application's memory area and maintain pointers to open files).

DOSspeak

FCBS=*x*[,*y*]

Variable or Option	Function
x	Specifies the maximum number between 1 and 255 (4 is the default) of file control blocks that DOS can have open at one time.
y	(Versions 4+) Specifies the number between 0 through 225 (the default is 0) of file control blocks that are protected from automatic closure. The y parameter must always be less than or equal to the x parameter.

More stuff

Don't fool around with the FCBS configuration command unless your application program puts a gun to your head and forces you to change the number of file control blocks. Most of the new programs use file handles (see the FILES configuration command) instead of FCBs, so you can relax.

FILES

Specifies the number of files that can be open at one time.

DOSspeak

```
FILES=x
```

where x specifies the maximum number between 8 and 255 (the default is 8) of files that can be open at one time.

Sample

Many of the more modern application programs require at least 20 files to be open at one time. To increase the files open to this number in your CONFIG.SYS file, you enter

```
files=20
```

INCLUDE

Includes the contents of one menu item within another on a startup menu that lets the user choose between multiple configurations in a single CONFIG.SYS file (available in DOS 6+ only).

DOSspeak

> **INCLUDE=***blockname*

where *blockname* specifies the name of the menu item (also known as a *configuration block*) whose commands that you want to include another menu item.

Sample

Suppose that you've created a startup menu that gives the user a choice between a basic configuration (called basic_config) and a standard configuration (called norm_config) when starting the computer. When defining the standard configuration menu item, you can include the commands already defined for the basic menu item by entering an INCLUDE command, such as the following, after the standard configuration block header (the name of the block enclosed in brackets).

```
[norm_config]
include=basic_config
```

Then, following this INCLUDE command, you place the rest of the configuration commands beyond those in the basic configuration that are unique to the standard configuration.

More stuff

For more information on defining multiple configurations in a single CONFIG.SYS file, see also MENUCOLOR, MENUDEFAULT, MENUITEM, and SUBMENU in this section.

INSTALL

Loads a memory-resident program into memory when you start your computer. These programs are also known as terminate-and-stay-resident (TSR) programs.

DOSspeak

> **INSTALL=**[*drive:*][*path*]***filename*** [*command-parameters*]

Variable or Option	Function
[*drive:*][*path*]*filename*	Specifies the drive, directory, and name of the memory-resident program to load. These programs routinely include FASTOPEN.EXE, KEYB.COM, NLSFUNC.EXE, and SHARE.EXE. If you omit the *drive:* and *path* parameters, DOS assumes the file is in the search path (see PATH in the DOS Commands section).
command-parameters	Specifies the parameters for the memory-resident program you are running.

Sample

To have DOS load the Norwegian keyboard program into memory for Cousin Olaf when he starts the computer, you enter

```
install=keyb.com no,865
```

in the CONFIG.SYS file.

More stuff

Place all INSTALL commands after the DEVICE commands in your CONFIG.SYS file because you can't load a memory-resident program before a device driver. Also, don't use INSTALL to load memory-resident programs that use environment variables, shortcut keys, or require COMMAND.COM to be present to handle errors.

LASTDRIVE

Specifies the maximum number of drives that DOS recognizes.

DOSspeak

```
LASTDRIVE=x
```

where *x* is the letter of the last drive on your computer (between A through Z). If you do not include a LASTDRIVE command in your CONFIG.SYS file, the last valid drive on your computer is the letter following the last drive in use. (So if the computer has a:, B:, C:, the default lastdrive is D.)

MENUCOLOR

Sets the text and background colors for the startup menu that lets the user choose between multiple configurations in a single CONFIG.SYS file (available in DOS 6 only).

DOSspeak

MENUCOLOR=x[, y]

Variable or Option	Function
x	Specifies the color of the menu text (between 0 and 15 — see the table that follows).
y	Specifies the color of the background screen (between 0 and 15 — see table below). If you omit the y parameter, DOS uses black for the background.

Your x and y parameters can be any of the parameters in the following table. When choosing x and y parameters, however, be sure that you select contrasting colors, or you won't be able to read your menu!

Value	Color	Value	Color
0	Black	8	Gray
1	Blue	9	Bright blue
2	Green	10	Bright green
3	Cyan	11	Bright cyan
4	Red	12	Bright red
5	Magenta	13	Bright magenta
6	Brown	14	Yellow
7	White	15	Bright white

More stuff

For more information on defining multiple configurations in a single CONFIG.SYS file, see also INCLUDE, MENUDEFAULT, MENUITEM, and SUBMENU in this section.

MENUDEFAULT

Specifies the default menu item for a startup menu that lets the user choose between multiple configurations in a single CONFIG.SYS file (available in DOS 6+ only).

DOSspeak

MENUDEFAULT=*blockname*[*,timeout*]

Variable or Option	Function
blockname	Specifies the name of the menu item that you want the startup menu to default to.
timeout	Specifies the number of seconds (between 0 and 90) that DOS waits before starting the computer with the default menu item specified by the *blockname* parameter. If you omit the *timeout* parameter, DOS uses a timeout of 0 seconds, which gives the user no chance ever to choose any of the other menu items — not too bright to give 'em options and then not allow them to choose.

Sample

Suppose that you've created a startup menu that gives the user a choice between using a basic configuration (called basic_config) and a standard configuration (called norm_config) when starting the computer. To make the standard configuration the default that DOS automatically uses if the user doesn't choose the basic one within 20 seconds, you enter

```
menudefault=norm_config,20
```

as the last command in the configuration block identified as [menu] that defines which menu items appear on the main menu (see MENUITEM for details).

More stuff

For more information on defining multiple configurations in a single CONFIG.SYS file, see also INCLUDE, MENUCOLOR, MENUITEM, and SUBMENU in this section.

MENUITEM

Specifies the menu items to be included in a startup menu that lets the user choose between multiple configurations in a single CONFIG.SYS file (available in DOS 6+ only).

DOSspeak

MENUITEM=*blockname*[, *menu_text*]

Variable or Option	Function
blockname	Specifies the name of the menu or submenu item that identifies what configuration commands are to be carried out when the user selects the menu item. If the MENUITEM command defines a main menu item, it must be located in the configuration block identified with the [menu] heading. If the MENUITEM command defines a submenu item, it must be located in the configuration block identified by the blockname used in the SUBMENU command. The configuration block containing the commands carried out when the user selects the menu item must then be defined elsewhere in the CONFIG.SYS file and identified with the *blockname* specified in the MENUITEM command enclosed in brackets. When the user chooses the menu item, DOS carries out all commands in this configuration block as well as all commands in a configuration block identified by the [common] heading.
menu_text	Specifies the text you want DOS to display after the menu number it assigns to the menu item (up to 70 characters).

Sample

To create a menu with two menu items that lets the user choose between a basic and a standard configuration, you enter

```
[menu]
menuitem=basic_config,Basic Configuration
menuitem=norm_config,Good Old Standard
     Configuration
```

Then, when you start your computer, DOS displays the following startup menu:

```
MS-DOS 6 Startup Menu
=======================
    1. Basic Configuration
    2. Good Old Standard Configuration
```

More stuff

For more information on defining multiple configurations in a single CONFIG.SYS file, see also INCLUDE, MENUCOLOR, MENUDEFAULT, and SUBMENU in this section.

NUMLOCK

Specifies whether the Num Lock key is set to on or off when you start your computer (available in DOS 6+ only).

DOSspeak

NUMLOCK=[on | off]

Variable or Option	Function
on	Turns on the Num Lock key when DOS displays the startup menu.
off	Turns off the Num Lock key when DOS displays the startup menu.

More stuff

NUMLOCK is one of the six new commands for defining startup menus and multiple configurations for your system. See also INCLUDE, MENUCOLOR, MENUITEM, and SUBMENU.

SHELL

Specifies the name and location of the command interpreter (COMMAND.COM unless you specify another).

DOSspeak

SHELL=[[*drive:*]*path*]***filename*** [*parameters*]

Variable or Option	Function
[[*drive:*]*path*]*filename*	Specifies the drive, directory, and name of the file containing the command interpreter. If you omit the *drive:* and *path* parameters, DOS looks in the root directory of the disk you boot from.
parameters	Specifies any command line parameters or switches that can be used with the command interpreter specified by the *filename* parameter.

More stuff

You don't need to add a SHELL command to your CONFIG.SYS file unless you've put the COMMAND.COM in some directory besides the root directory of the disk you boot from (drive C in almost all cases), or unless you want to use some other shell (that is, interface) you've cooked up or come across in your travels.

STACKS

Specifies the number and size of the data stacks used to handle hardware interrupts.

DOSspeak

STACKS=*n*,*s*

Variable or Option	Function
n	Specifies the number of stacks (0 or numbers between 8 and 64).
s	Specifies the size (in bytes) of each stack (0 or numbers between 32 and 512).

More stuff

The default settings for the STACKS commands are 0,0 for the IBM PC, IBM PC/XT, and IBM PC-Portable computers and 9,128 for all other computers.

Don't fool around with the STACKS command unless you're getting those wonderful Stack Overflow error messages before your computer bombs, your application program demands you to, or the devil makes you do it.

SUBMENU

Specifies a submenu item on a startup menu that, when chosen, displays a menu of further choices to the user. Startup menus are used to let the user choose between multiple configurations in a single CONFIG.SYS file (available in DOS 6+ only).

DOSspeak

SUBMENU=*blockname*[, *menu_text*]

Variable or Option	Function
blockname	Specifies the name of the submenu containing the menu items that are to be displayed when the user chooses the submenu item. The SUBMENU command must be located in the configuration block identified with the [menu] heading. The MENUITEM commands specifying the new menu items — to be displayed when the user selects the submenu item on the main menu — are placed in a separate configuration block identified with the *blockname* parameter specified in the SUBMENU command enclosed in brackets.
text	Specifies the text you want DOS to display after the menu number it assigns to the submenu item (up to 70 characters).

Sample

Suppose that you decide that, instead of defaulting to the standard configuration, when a user chooses the standard rather than the basic on the main menu, you'll offer a further choice: a submenu between an enhanced and the plain-vanilla standard configuration.

To do so, you enter

```
[menu]
menuitem=basic_config,Basic Configuration
submenu=standmenu,Standard Configuration
```

```
[standmenu]
menuitem=enhanc_config,Souped-Up Standard
    Configuration
menuitem=norm_config, Plain Old Standard
    Configuration
```

Then, when you start the computer, DOS displays the following startup menu on your screen:

```
MS-DOS 6 Startup Menu
=======================
    1. Basic Configuration
    2. Standard Configuration
```

When the user chooses option 2. Standard Configuration, DOS replaces the main menu with the following submenu of choices:

```
MS-DOS 6 Startup Menu
-----------------------
    1. Souped Up Standard Configuration
    2. Plain Old Standard Configuration
```

More stuff

For more information on defining multiple configurations in a single CONFIG.SYS file, see also INCLUDE, MENUCOLOR, MENUDEFAULT, and MENUITEM in this section.

SWITCHES

Does a number of wacky things, such as specifies that an enhanced keyboard work like an older keyboard, tells DOS that the WINA20.386 file has been moved out of the root directory, prevents you from using the F5 or F8 keys to bypass the startup command, or skips the two-second delay after displaying the DOS startup message.

DOSspeak

SWITCHES=[/k] [/w] [/n] [/f]

Variable or Option	*Function*
/k	Forces an enhanced (101-key) keyboard to act like an older (84-key) keyboard. This switch is used only when running an older program that can't deal with the enhanced keyboard arrangement.

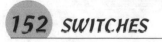

/w	Tells DOS that the WINA20.386 file has been moved to a directory other than the root directory so that you can run Windows 3.0 on a 386 computer. When you use this switch, your CONFIG.SYS file must also contain a DEVICE command indicating the correct whereabouts of the WINA20.386.
/n	Prevents you from using the F5 or F8 keys to bypass startup commands (not that you would anyway).
/f	Skips the two-second delay after displaying the Starting MS-DOS... message when you boot the computer.

More stuff

When using the SWITCHES command in your CONFIG.SYS file, you can combine the various switches in one file by separating each switch with a space as follows:

```
switches=/k /n /f
```

Index

A

A> prompt, 7

APPEND command, 8–9

    not to be used with BACKUP command, 13

ASSIGN command, 9–10

    not to be used with BACKUP command, 13

    not to be used with CHKDSK command, 16

    not to be used with FASTOPEN command, 53

    not to be used with JOIN command, 66

    not to be used with PRINT command, 95

    not to be used with SUBST command, 114

at sign (@) command, 128

ATTRIB command, 10–12

attributes, displaying or modifying for files, 10–12

AUTOEXEC.BAT file

    as batch file, 127

    enhancing prompts from, 97

    PATH command in, 92

B

backing up, files, 12–13, 89–90

BACKUP command, 12–13

    not to be used with SUBST command, 113

bar or pipe character (|), indicating choice of alternates, 3–4

batch files

    branching within, 128–129

    calling one from another, 128

    configuring for Ctrl-C or Ctrl-Break key press checks, 136

    displaying messages from, 130, 133–134

    parameter shifting, 134

    pausing execution, 133

    performing conditional processing, 132–133

    redirecting execution to specified line, 131

binary image files

    comparing, 53–55

    converting from EXE files, 49–50

boldface type, as used in this book, 3

brackets ([]), indicating optional parts of commands, 3

BREAK command, 136

buffers, allocating, 136

BUFFERS command, 136

C

E

F

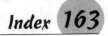

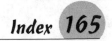

W

X

Order Form

Order Center: (800) 762-2974 (8 a.m.-5 p.m. PST, weekdays)
For fastest service, photocopy this order form and fax to: (415) 358-1260

Qty	ISBN	Title	Price	Total

Shipping & Handling Charges

Subtotal	U.S.	Canada & International	International Air Mail
Up to $20.00	Add $3.00	Add $4.00	Add $10.00
$20.01-40.00	$4.00	$5.00	$20.00
$40.01-60.00	$5.00	$6.00	$25.00
$60.01-80.00	$6.00	$8.00	$35.00
Over $80.00	$7.00	$10.00	$50.00

In U.S. and Canada, shipping is UPS ground or equivalent.
For Rush shipping call (800) 762-2974.

Subtotal	_____
CA residents add applicable sales tax	_____
IN residents add 5% sales tax	_____
Canadian residents add 7% GST tax	_____
Shipping	_____
TOTAL	_____

Ship to:

Name _____

Company _____

Address _____

City/State/Zip _____

Daytime Phone _____

Payment: ☐ Check to IDG Books (US Funds Only) ☐ Visa ☐ MasterCard ☐ AMEX

Card # _____ Exp. _____

Signature _____

Please send this order form to: IDG Books, 155 Bovet Road, Suite 310, San Mateo, CA 94402.
Allow up to 3 weeks for delivery. Thank you!

IDG BOOKS WORLDWIDE REGISTRATION CARD

RETURN THIS REGISTRATION CARD FOR FREE CATALOG

Title of this book: DOS For Dummies Quick Reference

My overall rating of this book: ❑ Very good [1] ❑ Good [2] ❑ Satisfactory [3] ❑ Fair [4] ❑ Poor [5]

How I first heard about this book:
❑ Found in bookstore; name: [6]
❑ Advertisement: [8]
❑ Word of mouth; heard about book from friend, co-worker, etc.: [10]
❑ Book review: [7]
❑ Catalog: [9]
❑ Other: [11]

What I liked most about this book:

What I would change, add, delete, etc., in future editions of this book:

Other comments:

Number of computer books I purchase in a year: ❑ 1 [12] ❑ 2-5 [13] ❑ 6-10 [14] ❑ More than 10 [15]

I would characterize my computer skills as: ❑ Beginner [16] ❑ Intermediate [17] ❑ Advanced [18] ❑ Professional [19]

I use ❑ DOS [20] ❑ Windows [21] ❑ OS/2 [22] ❑ Unix [23] ❑ Macintosh [24] ❑ Other: [25] _____ (please specify)

I would be interested in new books on the following subjects:
(please check all that apply, and use the spaces provided to identify specific software)

❑ Word processing: [26]
❑ Data bases: [28]
❑ File Utilities: [30]
❑ Networking: [32]
❑ Other: [34]
❑ Spreadsheets: [27]
❑ Desktop publishing: [29]
❑ Money management: [31]
❑ Programming languages: [33]

I use a PC at (please check all that apply): ❑ home [35] ❑ work [36] ❑ school [37] ❑ other: [38]

The disks I prefer to use are ❑ 5.25 [39] ❑ 3.5 [40] ❑ other: [41]

I have a CD ROM: ❑ yes [42] ❑ no [43]

I plan to buy or upgrade computer hardware this year: ❑ yes [44] ❑ no [45]

I plan to buy or upgrade computer software this year: ❑ yes [46] ❑ no [47]

Name: _____ Business title: [48]

Type of Business: [49]

Address (❑ home [50] ❑ work [51] /Company name: _____)

Street/Suite#

City [52] /State [53] /Zipcode [54]: _____ Country [55]

❑ **I liked this book!**
You may quote me by name in future IDG Books Worldwide promotional materials.

My daytime phone number is _____

IDG BOOKS
THE WORLD OF
COMPUTER
KNOWLEDGE

❏ YES!

Please keep me informed about IDG's World of Computer Knowledge. Send me the latest IDG Books catalog.